Creating a
Purposeful
Life

D1328681

"Richard's book is a superb contribution to the literature and will be of enormous benefit to everyone who wants to lead a deeper and more value-based life (and isn't that all of us!). Unusually he combines both wisdom and practicality with clarity. Strongly recommended."

Stephen Bampfylde, Director, Saxton Bampfylde,
Executive Search Boutique.

"A great workbook for life…This captures the essence of how to appreciate the value of our time and change for the better."

Dr Malcolm Parry OBE, Managing Director, Surrey Research Park.

"Richard Fox has written a timely treatise on a subject many people seldom take time to consider with any great depth – time itself and our relationship to it. It goes beyond simple 'time management' techniques to the core issues that determine how we experience life."

W. Bradford Swift, author of Spiral of Fulfilment: Living an Inspired Life of Service, Simplicity and Spiritual Serenity.

"I lead a happy and full life and manage my time fantastically, but I miss what I most admire about people who have made a difference to the world – 'a strong purpose'. This book is definitely the catalyst for me to define and live my purposeful life."

Niriti Mehta, Director Human Resources, Tebodin B.V.

"Many people, of all ages, are looking for greater meaning and purpose in their lives. This helpful guide shows the reader how to construct their own purposeful life and equally importantly how to put it all into practice."

Alastair Greeves, Director of Board Development – World Vision International

"*In Creating a Purposeful Life*, Richard Fox applies the NLP approach of modelling to find the 'differences that make a difference' in order to live well and fully. Richard shows how to live the deep truth that 'there is always enough time when you are in the present.'"

Robert Dilts, recognised internationally as one of the foremost developers,
trainers and practitioners of Neuro-Lingustic Programming.

Creating a
Purposeful
Life

*How to reclaim your life, live more
meaningfully and befriend time*

Richard Fox
with Heather Brown

The right of Richard Fox to be identified as the author of this book has been asserted in accordance with the Copyright, Designs and Patents Act 1988.

First published in 2012 by
Infinite Ideas Limited
36 St Giles
Oxford
OX1 3LD
United Kingdom
www.infideas.com

A CIP catalogue record for this book is available from the British Library

ISBN 978–1–906821–97–5

Cover designed by Cylinder
Text designed and typeset by Nicki Averill Design
Printed in Britain

'Hide not your talents. They for use were made. What's a sundial in the shade?'

Benjamin Franklin, American statesman, scientist, philosopher, inventor and writer.

My sincere thanks to all my contributors (over 120 of them), who are listed on page xiii, and to myriad others of many nationalities who, from my childhood onwards have helped shape my own philosophies on personal effectiveness, leadership and creating a Purposeful Life.

And my gratitude to my wife Sandi for her encouragement and support on this and so many other projects.

Contents

Preface

Time flies by

This book came into being as a result of my personal struggle with time. Although I had been using a time management system for 30 years and had facilitated many workshops on 'Using Time Effectively' I still felt that I was far from making the best use of each hour or each day.

I wanted to find out how others made use of their time and whether the experience of time seeming to fly by was a shared feeling. I sent out a brief questionnaire to over 300 people and got over 120 responses from 21 countries which were unique to each person, and at the same time identified themes that seem to concern many of us.

Reading the responses I realised that at the heart of my concern, and many other people's, about how to use time better is the desire to maximise unique gifts and talents and lead a Purposeful Life. The practical tips that the contributors offered helped me with the Purposeful Lives strand of my work, which I have been pursuing for the last 12 years.

Why read this book? What are its unique benefits?

This book is a practical guide full of tips on how to unearth your unique purpose in life and enjoy a better relationship with time. It is for you if you:

(a) Are starting to question the meaning and purpose of life or you are already sensing that time is flying by;

(b) Feel unfulfilled in your life and are considering a change of career;

(c) Are looking for practical tips on mindfulness and presence and building a balanced life;

(d) Are currently out of work and realise the importance of carrying out some 'internal research' to map out suitable career options.

This book will help you examine your current relationship with time, develop your own Purposeful Life action plan, overcome barriers to change, use your time more intentionally, re-plan your career and choose some ideas to sustain you on your journey. It pulls together the results of my own research and links to the work of other people. It is thought-provoking and practical at the same time, presented in small packages which can be digested individually or put together into a larger action plan.

Really engaging with the content of this book will help you to lead the life you were born to live. You could choose to ignore this opportunity, but who wants to end up as an 80 or 90 year-old mumbling 'If only... if only...'?

How to use this book

The book looks first at the practical problems of time, to help you identify what you want to change in your relationship with time and how to live life intentionally. Then we look at your unique gifts and talents, your core beliefs and values, the things that energise you, and your identity and spirit. This will enable you to map the main components of a Purposeful Life.

This is also a book for dipping into – start anywhere you like!

In most of the chapters I invite you to complete one or more exercises. You can either write your answers in this book in the spaces provided or you may prefer to use a separate journal or notebook.

Dip into ...

Chapter 1 to look at why time matters, why we feel time flies by and to summarise your current relationship with time.

Chapter 2 to discover the elements of a Purposeful Life and the structure of the Purposeful Life journey.

Chapter 3 to unearth your unique talents and core capabilities.

Chapter 4 to identify the beliefs and values that energise you.

Chapter 5 to explore your sense of who you are, your identity, and the legacy you want to build.

Chapter 6 to consider how your spirit connects you to the bigger picture.

Chapter 7 to bring everything together and create a map of your Purposeful Life.

Chapter 8 to see how you can use your map to start journeying towards a Purposeful Life.

Chapter 9 to explore the importance of being – doing is not enough.

Chapter 10 to find out how to anchor your being so that it supports your doing.

Chapter 11 to find tips for building being into your daily life.

Chapter 12 to find ideas about how to use your being to make your doing much more effective.

Chapter 13 to balance the other key dimensions of your Purposeful Life – your relationships with self and others.

Chapter 14 to find a model for enacting your plan – how to overcome barriers and make it real.

Chapter 15 for ideas on how to keep your momentum going to create the changes you want.

Chapter 16 for how you can use the Purposeful Lives approach to career planning.

Chapter 17 for provocative ideas for taking your thinking to the next level!

The Appendix for two worked examples of how to use the Six-Step Change Process to overcome personal barriers to change.

I hope this book will help you to set your own compass bearing and enable you to take your initial steps on your personal pathway.

Contributors

I am particularly grateful to Heather Brown, a wonderful friend and business associate, who has helped me enormously in putting this book together. I am also grateful to all of the research contributors: John Alderdice, Mahima Amin, David Apicella, Fred Ayres, Desmond Bain, Cim Bartlett, Mahnaz Bhatti, Georgia Black, Kimiko Bokura, Gavin Breeze, Kaaren Brook, Chaz Brooks, Heather Brown, Meike Bugler, Isabel Cabanis, Atiya Chaudrey, Sarah Christie, Lynn Chamberlain Clark, Kate Cobb, Vincent Cornelius, Ian Crocker, Sharon Croome, Stephen Cutler, David Dadswell, Mark Darby, Mike Davies, Gino D'Ippolito, Lukasz Dobromirski, Ron Down, Paul Engel, Morfydd Evans, Fran Everist, Julie Farrar, Charlotte Fenton, Jock Gardner, Peter Godber, John Gooding, Peter Goryalov, Alastair Greeves, Kim Gregory, Tom Hall, Alan Harpham, Rabbe Hedengren, Sue Howard, Brian Howden, Ash Idnani, Katalin Illes, Branka Ljamic Ivanovic, Carl Jackson, Bryan Johnston, Deidre Glynne Jones, Win King, Joseph Lahue, Ray Lamb, Peter Levell, Louise Lloyd, Michael Lofthouse, Tim Lucas, Belinda Macdonald, Tim Marks, Alwyn Marriage, Christopher Mayfield, Lesley Meyer, Gary Miles, Stuart Mitchell, John Nelson, Audrey Nice, Joy Nix, Louise Nix, Angela O'Connell, Hilary Oliver, Christina Osborne, Patricia Overland, Jane Ozanne, Dennis Packham, Ruth Paris, ChiHyun Park, Claire Pedrick, Anna Pensante, Felicia Perseguer, John Phillip, Gillian Pickering, Christina Ponds, Lesley Pugh, James Ramsay, John Remynse, Nic Robinson, Martin Rodler, David Rohrer, Ilja van Roon, Frans Sandbergen, Deborah Seabrook, Alister Scott, Nicky Slater, Emma Scott-Smith, Belinda Smith, Martin Smith, Ingrid Terry, Diana Thrush, Amy Ting, John Truscott, Rutton Viccajee, Bernie Wales, Ian Walsh, Jeff Ward, Rosie Ward, Kathyrn Weiss, Elizabeth Welch, Marc Wethmar, Joni

Shepard Wickline, Barbara Wietasch, Keith Williams, Mike Wilson, Howard Worsley, Neja Zupan.

Richard Fox

Farnham Castle, Surrey, England, December 2011

Part 1

Part 1

1 Why does time matter?

Most of us have an ambiguous relationship with time. In our fast moving society, most people feel they don't have enough time – but can we do something about that?

There are so many demands on us. Life in colleges and in the work place is pressured. We can feel overwhelmed by the flood of information bearing down on us. And thank goodness inanimate objects can't speak otherwise we would hear them shouting: 'When are you going to cut the lawn, tidy the garage, clean the car, repaint the dining room?' We can also feel guilty that we are not spending more time with family and friends or actually doing the hobbies that we list on our CVs.

Many people seem to feel that they are spending too much time:	And not enough time:
Doing – hamster wheel busy-ness	Being
Living in the past/future	Living in the present moment
Continuously striving	Being content
Rushing ahead	Living a Purposeful Life
Observing time flying by	Gazing, savouring each minute
Regarding time as an enemy	Befriending time
Being the runner-up in the rat race	Leading life at their own pace

In order to explore the practical problems of time, the questionnaire I sent out to over 300 people of different religions and over 21 nationalities included these questions:

1. Do you think time flies by? If 'yes' why? If 'no' why not?

2. What specifically is happening within you on days when you feel you are making the most of time?
3. Can you share a practical tip, saying, prayer, poem, thought or practice that others might find helpful in slowing down time's spinning top?

Why bother wrestling with questions like these? Because they have practical consequences for the way we live our lives. Does everyone find certain activities a drag on time, and others time enriching? Does everyone find the same activities time-dragging, or is it unique to each person? What is it that makes an activity time enriching?

Here's what one of my research contributors said about the problem of time:

> I think that the 'problem' of time – not having enough, it passing too quickly, feeling overwhelmed by life's events – is one of **relationship** and **attention**. By **relationship** I mean the way we consciously relate to the world of external events and our own inner world. And much of this relating is evaluative rather than experiential. To put it in more practical terms: most people spend their energy thinking about how things should have been, could have been or can/will/ought etc to be. Whatever happens, the thing inside we call 'I' has an opinion, association, memory or any other mental construct that consumes much of our attention.

> And in this lies the second part of the problem: our **attention**. Our attention is not usually with the Thing or Event itself, but with our reflection or evaluation of it. This creates a distance between us and the world, our thinking and our being. Rather than living our life, we plan it. Rather than experience something, we get lost in thought about that experience. The connection is lost and in that loss we exchange joyful living for constant concern that 'time is running out'.

Most of us have times when we wonder:
- 'What's the point?'
- 'What am I here for?'
- 'Am I making the best use of my time?'

This may be to do with the money you want to earn, the places you want to visit, the experiences you want to have, or your desire to have a sense of meaning and purpose in your life.

You might like to do a quick ranking of those drivers before you read further, and add any extra ones which are important to you. As I ordered my own drivers, I realised that the key, core one was having a sense of purpose and meaning, and I made a link to the work on Purposeful Lives that I have been engaged in for the last 12 years.

I realised that if I was going to live more intentionally, then I needed to understand why certain activities are time-enrichers for me and how they are connected to what I believe to be my purpose: the reason I'm on this planet.

I found an echo of this in the piece written by one of my contributors:

> Time shows its natural slowness when I'm really connected to the higher, subtler meaning of our being human, here, now, when my existence flows from my deepest core, the 'tender soft spot'. True connection to another human being, to the soul of nature: that's the place where time is meaningful and I can accept it, going beyond it. All the rest is more or less artificial, constructed, a projection of my conscious mind that sometimes makes life feel unreal.

> They say: 'Time is Money'. I like to think: 'Time is Love'. Being in love with life, even when she shows me her ugliest, dirtiest face, is the only way to spend this priceless treasure that somebody has lent us for one occasion only – time.

What most of us want is not only to stop feeling guilty about how we currently use time but to actually live a Purposeful Life. This means that we need to dig deeper than time management techniques in order to understand what our Purposeful Life would look like. We need to consider our unique talents and key capabilities and what beliefs and values energise and inspire us. Then our Purposeful Life will be in line with the identity we want to create for ourselves, with our spirit awakening and inspiring us to lead the life we were born to live.

What my research contributors said about time

Here is a summary of the main reasons my research contributors think time flies by. Which ones are true for you?

Why time flies by

The pace of modern life – *Our way of life has accelerated over recent decades.*
- The communication 'takeover' by email and internet.
- Ever-increasing choices and multiple leisure opportunities.
- Hanging on the phone for someone to 'get back to you'.
- Filling in forms, endless bureaucracy, waiting in line.

Too much to do – *I seldom have time to do all that I undertake.*
- Days fly quickly away in a crazy run.
- I'm living not in today, but some weeks ahead.
- Every time I start to read something I immediately start glancing at the pile of other things awaiting my attention.

Getting older – *Life is like a holiday. The second half goes much faster than the first.*
- As children we are constantly experiencing completely new things. However, as we get older we do not come across many different things.

- When we are young we are much less conscious of our own mortality; time is a commodity which we can take for granted.
- We try to hold time back and thus we focus on it slipping by.

Our unique view of time – Since our thinking minds make time, we also make it either long or short.

- There is little in the outside world we influence and even less we control.
- Most people say time flies. The exceptions are the elderly or those who are sick and unable to be active.
- We all know that if we are waiting a minute is too long, if we are enjoying ourselves a minute is nothing.

Understanding your own relationship with time in more depth

Time management books take the view that time is a scarce resource that needs to be used productively. But this is not the only way of viewing time. If you want to change the way you use your time, you need a deeper understanding of your present relationship with it.

Use these more detailed descriptions, based on what my research contributors said to help form your own summary of how you relate to time.

For disappearing acts, it's hard to beat what happens to the eight hours supposedly left after eight of sleep and eight of work.

Doug Larson

Many people said that they are 'busy' people; they always have lots to do and seldom have enough time to do all they undertake so time flies by. It can feel as though we are living in the future, not in the present – days fly quickly away following one another, from morning to evening, in a crazy run. We develop the habit of trying to do too much. Despite a wealth of experience that shows that invariably things take longer than expected, we still start too many things at once and then get frustrated that they are moving forward more slowly than we would like.

How do we know whether we're being productive as we race through time? Do you recognise these danger signs? 'I don't have time to eat, drink or blow my nose, and each time I start to read something that I should have read ages ago, I immediately start glancing at the pile of other things that are awaiting my attention.'

The trouble with our times is that the
future is not what it is used to be.
Paul Valery

Why does time seem to go past faster than it used to? Is it to do with modern society and communications? Our way of life has accelerated over recent decades with huge increases in the numbers and use of cars, the communication 'takeover' by the internet, email and texting, increasing pressures and expectations in the workplace, ever-increasing choices with consumer pressures and multiple leisure opportunities. We spend a lot of our time waiting in for delivery drivers or repair men, filling in forms, waiting in line. How much time do we really have left for ourselves?

Or perhaps it comes from inside us – perhaps it's to do with the way our brains work. The stream of information coming from the outside world is constantly increasing. The second stream emerges from within us (e.g. ideas, intuitive feelings). As we start processing it, our environment continues to inundate us with more information, so our mind often feels like a mouse or hamster on a treadmill – running against time and always lagging behind.

> Men talk of killing time, while time
> quietly kills them.
> **Dion Boucicault**

Perhaps time flying by has something to do with our age. Do you have a memory like this one?

> I remember being 12 years old, sitting on my front driveway in July, enjoying the cool concrete, as I sat and watched my street come alive. It was just a few quiet moments before a busy summer day. What I remember most was the feeling that my summer was stretching endlessly before me – full of possibilities. Now 30 years later I rush through my days, gulp a cup of coffee down while answering an email and talking on the phone to a client or co-worker.

Time seems to fly faster the older you get. As we put up the Christmas tree and decorations, it seems only a few days since we were last doing it, yet it's a whole year! Why is this? Perhaps time flies by because we measure our lives in years, and the older you get, the smaller the proportion a year becomes of your life overall. When you can look back to something 20 or 30 years ago, what happened a year ago seems very recent. When you are 5, a year represents one-fifth of your life, whereas when you are 50, it is just one-fiftieth.

Perhaps the reason time goes more quickly as we get older is because we do not come across so many completely new things – everything has some familiarity. As children we are constantly experiencing new things; because so many new and different things are happening to us we feel like a lot has happened.

Time is broken down more, giving the illusion of it being slower. Or perhaps as we become more mature, we are more in control of our lives than when we were younger and that makes time pass more quickly.

> Time is a great teacher, but unfortunately
> it kills all its pupils.
> **Louise Hector Berlioz**

Time may seem to pass more quickly because when we are young we are much less conscious of our own mortality. As one of our contributors said, 'Life is like your holiday. The second half goes much faster than the first.' It is thought that urgency is connected to mortality; finite, ever-shortening life means we focus on the urgency, and time seems to speed up. There is a sense that there is something out there that we're supposed to be doing, and that we're running out of time to work out what it is.

> Time is an illusion – lunchtime doubly so.
> **Douglas Adams**

We always have so many things on our to-do lists, so many people to talk to, so many plans to realise. This is typical for people in a Western society – it might be very different if we lived a different life style, in a different job, in a different country. People in different countries perceive time differently – Fons Trompenaars, in his book *The Cross Cultural Continuum*, talks about the fact that linear time is a very European notion; in the Middle East and Asia, time is much more relaxed. In my experience of working in different countries it seems that Germans, Spaniards and Swedes have different ideas about what is meant by 'arriving on time' for a meeting.

Time flies by differently for people in different circumstances. If we were in prison and the use of our time were not under our own control, would it seem to pass more slowly?

It appears that the rate at which time passes is related to what we are doing and how much we enjoy that activity. The more we are spending time pleasurably or rewardingly, the faster it seems to go; we are absorbed and therefore not conscious of the passage of time. Conversely, when we are engaged in a less fulfilling/unpleasant activity time can seem to drag. In a painful situation, the time passes even more slowly. And sometimes, just sometimes, time almost stands still:

> I was 16 years old in the middle of the handball game. I was clearly in the "flow" state; I saw all the opponents moving in slow motion, and I was able to move so quickly ahead of their moves.

Time goes, you say? Ah, no!
Alas – time stays, we go.
Henry Austin Dobson

Who decides how we experience time?

If our sense of time is created by us, it is our personal responsibility. Our experience of time is personal and embodied and so can't be separated from us.

What can happen is that we lose track of time; our body can track time at a different rate from the machine time of clocks and calendars. Losing track of time can be positive, e.g. when we find calm silence through meditation or negative, e.g. when we miss an appointment because we got sidetracked by an incoming phone call. Either way it helps to remind us that our experience of time is something we are responsible for.

The challenge of really accepting that our sense of time is our own responsibility is vividly thrown down in *The Compass of Zen* by Seung Sahn, Korean Zen Master: 'Time is not long or short…. since our thinking minds make time, we also make it either long or short. If you practise meditation, however, you can actually perceive that in one moment, there is infinite time. In one moment, there is infinite space. In one moment, there is everything! One moment is endless time and space….'

Metaphors about time

I have two metaphors for time:

- 'Time is like the sand in an egg timer: time cannot be reversed.'
- 'Time is like standing on a railway platform when a non-stop express train rushes past – it is gone in a flash.'

But my desired relationship with time is like that of a slow flowing river full of sparkling life and interest.

I asked my contributors for their metaphors about time. Notice the fundamentally different ways they regard time, underlining the fact that we create our own structure of time. Which metaphor(s) do you relate to? They may help you as you summarise your own relationship with time.

Time as water

Time is like a dripping tap. It seems really slow when you concentrate on it, but it fills a bowl really quickly when you look away.

Time is like an ocean on which we sail, whose courses and landing places are virtually infinite.

Time is like a ruthless ocean.

Time is like a flowing river – its flow can't be stopped, its current is changeable, you can relax and let it carry you or you can fight and swim upstream.

Time is like water, it flows everywhere.

Time is like a rainbow, precious, untouchable, and gone too soon.

Time as space

Time is like a spiral.

Time is a vortex.

Time as life rhythm

Time is like a runaway train.

Time is like a walk in the park; we can rush by or watch the flowers growing.

Time is like a ticking clock, however we don't hear the ticking anymore.

Time is like a huge balloon, when it is deflated, it needs lots of energy to fill it up again.

Time is like my best girl friend, comes and goes without saying.

(When related to my work) Time is like a crushing machine ruining our structured high quality work.

The relativity of time

Time is like a melody – play it in tune and you journey in harmony. Play it out of tune and you get a bumpy ride.

Time can stand still or be fleeting. Time is both elusive and tangible.

Quotations about the problem of time

Times change and we (change) with them.
From a Latin Proverb

Put your hand on a hot stove for a minute, and it seems like an hour.
Sit with a pretty girl for an hour, and it seems like a minute. THAT'S
relativity.
Albert Einstein

Lunchtime 'al fresco' has been replaced by 'al desko'.
Richard Fox

How do YOU experience time?

You might like to record your reactions to these first chapters, and ask
yourself some questions about your own current relationship with time.

Does time fly by for you?

Is that good or bad? Is there something else you would like to say about that?

What are you noticing right now about how you feel you have used the
time spent reading this chapter? Are you feeling the need to evaluate
whether it was useful or not, did your attention just float in and out,
alighting on the jewels that appealed to you?

What are you noticing, and what does it tell you about how you experience and use time?

_____

What deeper questions is this bringing up for you?

_____

I guess that you have been wrestling with this thing called 'time' for several years and that some of the thoughts I have shared with you echo your own experiences. Your situation, however, is unique.

So before we look at how other people construct their Purposeful Lives, I invite you to write down your vision of the relationship you personally want with time. You can amend and enhance it later.

You might find what I'm about to ask a bit 'off the wall' or plain daft, but I invite you to stop what you are doing and listen to your body. What is your body telling you right now about what your ideal relationship with time should be?

My vision of my ideal relationship with time is…

2 Time and the elements of a Purposeful Life

Why does the fact that time flies by matter to me? When I dig beneath the surface to look for an answer I find that it is an issue for me because I want to make something of my life. Life is not some sort of rehearsal. I'm only on this planet once, so what do I need to investigate to find greater meaning and purpose in my life? Perhaps then I will be able to make the contribution in the world that only I can make.

To explore this, I invite you to consider the questions I thought about in order to understand my own Purposeful Life:

- What is it about me that is unique? What is my 'difference that makes the difference'?
- What motivates and energises me?
- What would my Purposeful Life look like, if it were based on my unique talents and skills and my core beliefs and values?
- What beneficial shifts can I make in my relationship with time so that time can increasingly become a friend rather than an enemy?

Looking at the diagram below, most time management techniques try to take us directly round the perimeter from 1 to 5, bypassing the inner work of 2 to 4; that's why they are so difficult to sustain.

We need to dig deeper, to go to the centre of ourselves in order to unearth our purpose; only then can we start working outwards again to create a more purposeful, intentional life and the relationship with time that we really want.

This 'inside-out' approach is summarised in the following diagram:

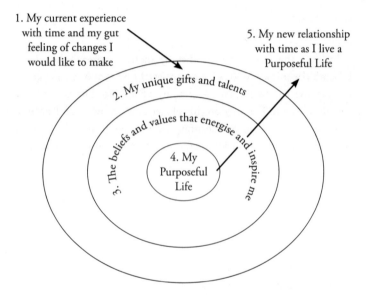

1. My current experience with time and my gut feeling of changes I would like to make

5. My new relationship with time as I live a Purposeful Life

2. My unique gifts and talents

3. The beliefs and values that energise and inspire me

4. My Purposeful Life

I found myself asking: how would having a greater understanding of (a) my unique gifts, talents and key capabilities; (b) the beliefs and values that energise me; (c) who I wish to become, and my connection with the 'bigger picture' help me become clearer about the purpose of my life? Then how would I need to reallocate my time to live a Purposeful Life?

Very few personal development courses and coaching programmes get to the essence, the core of who we really are: to the deep, personal and private territory of our top 3–4 unique talents and strengths, our beliefs and values, our identity and spiritual connections. Put another way, we are like an iceberg with only our physical appearance and possessions, our behaviours and some of our capabilities appearing above the waterline. Other factors making up who we are and who we might wish to become are hidden from view under the waterline. I have illustrated this in the following diagram, later I will explain what these captions mean.

On several occasions I have worked with Robert Dilts (http://www. robertdilts.com). Some years ago Robert developed a model called the Logical Levels of Experience. He suggests that we all operate at six different levels, but that we do not necessarily pay attention to all of these levels or recognise their inter-relationships.

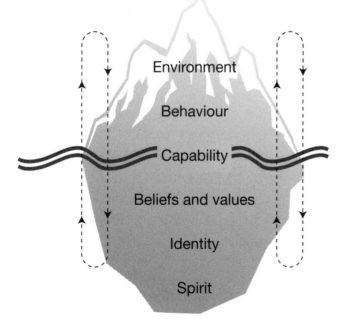

I notice in my own life that when all the Logical Levels are working well together in and through me, then I experience a state of 'flow' or 'alignment' and these are occasions when I feel that I am truly living a Purposeful Life.

You may want to use the following table as a starting point to consider this in more detail. Start at the top of the model (i.e. the bit of the iceberg that is above the water!) and work your way down, noticing the strong inter-relationships between levels. Then review your current situation in relation to each of the six levels in turn. This may help you to identify where any misalignment, de-energising or dissatisfaction is currently taking place.

Level	Typical questions	
Environment	The realm of most personal development and time management processes.	What possessions and relationships do I need to fulfil my purpose in life?
Behaviours	What? When? Where?	What am I doing that I could do in a smarter way, or stop doing?
Capabilities	How?	How can I optimise my potential?
Beliefs and Values	Why?	Why am I on this planet?
Identity	Who?	Who do I wish to become to fulfil my mission, my purpose in life?
Spirit	For what? With whom/what?	In what ways do I feel connected to something/ someone bigger than myself? What is my vision?

What are your most urgent questions right now?

Some years ago I decided to focus my professional work on 'Purposeful Lives' and 'Purposeful Organisations', believing that if I can help individuals and organisations to become clear about their identity, their core beliefs, values and strengths then most day-to-day concerns would be resolved more easily resulting in greater alignment, productivity and fulfilment.

In order to define our own Purposeful Life I believe we need to adopt an 'inside-out' approach by first examining the levels that are normally hidden from public view. These are the four levels under the waterline in the iceberg diagram.

To help you map your own unique Purposeful Life based on these levels, I encourage you to spend time considering what is really important to you, at each of the four key levels. The next four chapters explore each level in more detail, and give you specific questions to consider. In order to really notice what matters to you, you need to take time to reflect on the questions, so I suggest that you don't try to complete all four chapters in one sitting – you risk getting indigestion!

Instead, take them one at a time, and notice which chapters energise you and which ones you find harder. Within each chapter, try to answer all of the questions, but you may notice that one question jumps out as key, and that you don't really need to answer the others, because everything is summed up by one question in particular.

Have fun!

3 My unique gifts, talents and key capabilities

When I work with individuals and groups I am often asked why I decided to specialise in leadership and other aspects of personal development. When replying, I say that for many years I have been fascinated by the fact that each of us is unique. We have unique finger prints, eyes, ear lobes and DNA. The way we filter all the information we receive differs from one person to another. As Stephen Covey, author of *The Seven Habits of Highly Effective People*, says: 'We see the world not as it is, but as we are – or, as we have been conditioned to see it.'

More importantly, each one of us has a unique story to tell based on the knowledge and experience we have acquired.

I believe that there are some profound reasons why each one of us is unique. If we are to live our lives to the full we need to:

(a) Unearth the treasures which are our unique gifts and talents and then think about who we wish to become. We might refer to this as our vocation or 'calling'.
(b) Bring these treasures into the world to the maximum extent possible. Martha Graham, one of the founders of modern dance refers to this as 'keeping your channel open'.

You are only on this planet once. So why not spend a day or so unearthing your unique talents, gifts and strengths, identifying the unique contribution that you could make to society and in your work? If you choose to burn yourself up, let it be the result of being and doing something really worthwhile, rather than just the result of being busy. You have the potential to become the difference that makes THE difference.

If you really take on board the fact that you are unique, you can choose to opt out of the rat race, create your own personal pathway and move along it at your own speed – you can take charge of your relationship with time. You may still continue to be busy but you will know that what you are engaged in is meaningful, fulfilling and aligned to your inner core. Knowing this, you can learn techniques to enrich every hour and slow down your internal clock. Incidentally, organisations would be transformed if they helped their people unearth their unique talents and strengths and then made every effort to enable their people to use these gifts each day.

You would fill many pages if you listed all the things you can do and all the topics you are knowledgeable about. For the purpose of this book my definition of Key Capabilities is: of all the many things you know and can do, what are your top 3–4 core talents, gifts and strengths? Also, believing that 'the sky is the limit' what is your potential?

Just imagine for a moment that you are holding a large sieve and you are panning for gold. Now put all your accumulated knowledge and skills into this sieve and give it a jolly good shake until it is nearly empty. Now imagine that you are left with 3–5 golden nuggets. Each one represents one of your unique talents, gifts and strengths. It is probable that you will not know how or when you acquired at least one of these gifts. It may seem that you were born with it even if neither of your parents displayed this strength. How are you going to make the most of these precious nuggets?

There are several ways you can unearth your unique talents and strengths. For example you could, working with a friend or by yourself:

(a) Consider looking at free resources on the internet such as http://www.viacharacter.org/Surveys/SurveyCenter.aspx and then look at the summary questions 15 onwards below; and/or

(b) Ask yourself some high level questions such as questions 1–7 below; and/or

(c) Complete the lengthier exercise outlined in questions 8–14 below.

Use another sheet of paper to give yourself plenty of space to expand on your answers.

High level questions

1. What were your favourite childhood pastimes/hobbies?

2. Nowadays, what do you really enjoy doing?

3. What activities are you engaged in when you are at your very best?

4. What energises you?

5. What can you learn or do easily that others find more difficult?

_____

6. What do you dislike doing?

_____

7. Reviewing 1–6 above, what are your core talents and strengths?

_____

Now go to question 15

Longer exercise questions

8. List your top 30–50 achievements/things you were proud of from all aspects of your life, from childhood onwards.

_____

9. What particular knowledge and skills did you use to achieve 8?

_____

10. Which achievements gave you the greatest joy?

_____

11. What do others say you are good at?

_____

12. When you have a list of tasks to do, which one(s) do you want to do first because you enjoy doing them?

_____

13. Which tasks do you avoid?

_____

14. Summary: What themes emerge from the above?

_____

Now go to question 15

Summary questions

15. What insights have you gained about your Key Capabilities from answering the above questions?

16. In future what talent/strength do you want to use less or even stop using?

17. Which talents/parts of yourself would you love to use, but haven't yet had the chance to employ?

18. Which aspects of your character do you want to use more of in future?

19. In summary, putting any barriers/blockers to one side, what top 3–5 talents and strengths do you want to take into your future?

4 The values and beliefs that energise and guide us

Our values inform the way in which we operate our lives on a daily basis. Values that are important to us might include openness, trustworthiness and fairness. Following is a list of values, and also qualities or characteristics we might value. Scan the list, highlighting only those words that jump out at you, that give you a strong gut reaction as being important to you. Then gradually edit the list down, until you have the 3–7 values or qualities which are the most crucial to the type of life you want to live.

Some possible values

Acceptance	Contact with people	Expertise
Accomplishment	Cooperation	Fairness
Accuracy	Courage	Fame
Achievement	Creativity	Family
A Sense of Adventure	Decisiveness	Flexibility
Attractiveness	Dedication	Freedom
Awareness	Devotion	Friendship
Autonomy	Dignity	Fulfilment
Beauty	Discovery	Fun
Change	Education	Grace
Comfort	Encouragement	Guidance
Communicativeness	Elegance	Happiness
Community	Empathy	Harmony
Compassion	Enthusiasm	Health
Competition	Excellence	Helpfulness
Concentration	Excitement	Honesty
Connectedness	Experimentation	Humour

Imagination	Passion	Simplicity
Independence	Peace	Sociability
Influence	Perseverance	Solitude
Innovativeness	Persuasiveness	Spirituality
Inspiration	Playfulness	Spontaneity
Integration	Pleasure	Status
Integrity	Positivity	Success
Intimacy	Power	Thoroughness
Intuition	Pragmatism	Trust
Inventiveness	Precision	Uniqueness
Joy	Problem solving	Variety
Justice	Recognition	Versatility
Leadership	Responsibility	Vision
Liveliness	Risk	Vitality
Logic	Routine	Vocation/purpose
Love	Security	Wisdom
Mastery	Self-discipline	Zest
Modesty	Self-reliance	
Motivation	Sensitivity	*Add any other values*
Openness	Sensuality	*that are important to*
Order	Service	*you that are not on the*
Originality	Sharing	*above list*

My top 3–7 values are:

Our beliefs are principles, statements, assumptions or opinions which we might not be able to prove but which are really important to us and provide guidelines and boundaries for our lives.

Beliefs link what is important to us to the outside world e.g. 'I believe that in order to be happy I have to work hard.' Beliefs change over time. For example, 'I believed in Father Christmas until the Tooth Fairy told me he didn't exist!'

It is worth checking our core beliefs because they are, in the main, emotionally held opinions and assumptions. So they can be changed if we discover that one of them is incorrect, incomplete or no longer helpful.

Have a look at the following questions about your beliefs. Write your answers on a separate sheet of paper or in your journal so that you have plenty of space to expand on your ideas.

1. What are your beliefs about your:
(a) Living accommodation
(b) Personal financial position
(c) Personal possessions
(d) Partner and immediate family
(e) Choice of friends
(f) Job
(g) Education, knowledge base and skills
(h) Yourself
(i) Your self worth/self esteem/self confidence
(j) The Divine

2. What else is very important to you?

3. What are the things that motivate/drive you? It could perhaps be the things that pull you towards a particular goal or cause you to move away from your deepest fear.

4. What self limiting beliefs tend to hold you back e.g. I'm useless at maths/ learning languages?

5. Other than a self limiting belief (see above) is there any other belief or assumption you would like to change?

---

6. Summary:
What are your main insights from working through these questions?

If you would like to engage in a deeper exploration of what motivates and drives you, I suggest you begin with David McClelland's book *Human Motivation.*

In summary, McClelland proposed that human beings comprise three basic drivers: Achievement, Affiliation and Power. We learn these three drivers in our childhood and one driver tends to become more dominant than the other two. Within groups of people we are likely to get individuals with different primary drivers. Even though the group may include a few people with the same primary driver e.g. achievement, on closer study you notice that this manifests itself differently within each person, underlining the fact that each one of us is unique.

So what drives your behaviour and how does this affect how you spend your time?

5 Identity – my sense of who I wish to become

Our identity, in the context of this book, is much deeper than the physical characteristics by which we are recognised, the roles we play in life and what is occupying our mind. When these are stripped away, who am I and who do I wish to become? And equally importantly, what sort of person do I not want to become? Linking back to my beliefs, what are my boundaries?

> This above all: to thine own self be true,
> And it must follow, as the night the day,
> Thou canst not then be false to any man.
> **Polonius in *Hamlet*, Shakespeare**

The way I became clearer about my own identity, the essence of who I am and my mission in life was to work through the following list of verbs.

Pull out the verbs from the list that excite you. This list is not exhaustive, so add any other verbs that resonate with you.

From this list select the three most important. These three verbs are those which could help you shape your future activities. Then ask yourself:

- In what ways are these three verbs connected?
- What is the common theme?
- What are the linkages between these three verbs and any other verbs I shortlisted?
- How might I present pictorially the essence of who I am and my mission in life?

Some possible elements of your identity and mission

Adopt	Enlighten	Play
Advance	Enlist	Possess
Affect	Entertain	Prepare
Alleviate	Enthuse	Present
Amplify	Evaluate	Produce
Appreciate	Excite	Promote
Ascend	Explore	Provide
Bestow	Extend	Pursue
Brighten	Facilitate	Receive
Build	Finance	Reduce
Cause	Foster	Refine
Choose	Franchise	Relate
Claim	Further	Relax
Collect	Gather	Rely
Command	Grant	Remember
Communicate	Heal	Renew
Compel	Hold	Resonate
Compete	Illuminate	Revise
Compose	Implement	Sacrifice
Conceive	Improve	Satisfy
Confirm	Inspire	Sell
Construct	Integrate	Serve
Contact	Involve	Stand
Continue	Keep	Summon
Create	Labour	Support
Decide	Launch	Take
Defend	Lead	Tap
Delight	Light	Team
Demonstrate	Make	Trade
Devise	Manifest	Travel
Discover	Master	Understand
Direct	Motivate	Utilise
Draft	Mould	Validate
Dream	Move	Value
Drive	Nurture	Venture
Embrace	Open	Work
Encourage	Organise	Worship
Endow	Participate	Write
Enhance	Persuade	

Also consider having a look at these questions:

_____

Are you acting out your own life or an inherited life i.e. following someone else's script?

_____

How authentic are you in each area of your life?

_____

Who would you wish to become if you had no fear?

_____

If you had all the support you need who/what would you really like to be/do?

_____

Summary:

(a) What aspects of the identity you desire do you already have?

(b) What two things about your identity would you want to change, and which are changeable? i.e. not your height!

(c) How would you describe your present and desired identity, using a symbol or graphical/metaphorical language? (e.g. what sort of animal are you/would you like to be – and why?)

_____

6 Spirit – my connections to a bigger picture

Earlier we defined our spirit dimension as ways in which we feel connected to something bigger than ourselves. Examples of this are a feeling of connection with history, the stars at night, nature, a religious belief, a particular physical location, and certain types of music. Questions that might help you to get a sense of your spirit dimension are:

- What inspires or awakens me?
- What gives me a source of wonder, awe, joy?
- What is my ultimate purpose; my vision, my destiny?

Which of the following statements fit you best? How does this affect your connection to the bigger picture?

- I believe in the resurrected life and spending eternity in heaven.
- I believe in reincarnation.
- When I die, that's it, nothing follows.
- I believe in something bigger than me that's out there and benign.
- I believe in a unifying energy that flows from the universe through me.
- I believe that we are all holographic representations of the Divine.
- I believe that the only thing we can know is what science tells us about the universe.

My contributors shared many thoughts about how they see themselves in relation to the bigger picture. You might find some of their ideas useful as you explore this section.

If we value ourselves on the basis of what we do, we start running around like chickens without a head. When we accept that we are who we are and that things are as they are, we are less likely to believe that time is some kind of actual and limited resource that determines our fate.

Do not plan the future, live in the present. Live now. Worry is a waste of energy and a denial of faith.

Is the way you earn your living simply a 'job' or are you engaged in a worthwhile activity where you sense that you are truly making a difference? As individuals we decide if we have properly invested or wastefully squandered the time we have. It's all in our perception of the choices we make about how to use the same amount of time everyone in the world has.

As long as you are aware that you can master your life, your agenda, your time, then you are on a good road. If you still believe that you are dependent on the agendas/decisions of others, then it gets difficult!

'Man who treats life like a race gets
to the end very quickly'!
Confucius

Most people never realise they have choices, and squander their time on the unnecessary rather than the important stuff.

If we do not take time out to dream and think about what we would like to attract into our lives we are likely to end up getting what we do not necessarily want.

Now you might like to consider these questions:

1. In what circumstances do you feel connected to a 'bigger picture?'

---

2. If you had all the material possessions you need and yet felt something was missing in your life, what would it be?

---

3. What meaning and purpose do you want for your life?

---

4. What could be/is your unique contribution? 'Your difference that could make the difference?'

---

5. What do you want the rest of your life to be about?

_____

6. What legacy do you want to leave? What stories will your children or grandchildren tell about you?

_____

Summary: What difference does your connection with spirit make to the way you want to live your life and use your time?

_____

7 Summarising your Purposeful Life map

We shall not cease from exploration
And the end of all our exploring
Will be to arrive where we started
And know the place for the first time.
'Little Gidding', T.S Eliot

You have now had the opportunity to explore questions about your Purposeful Life at four levels: key capabilities, beliefs and values, identity and spirit.

As you were answering these questions you probably remembered situations when you were at your very best and in a state of 'flow' or 'alignment'. For a powerful example of alignment across all the levels, and a model of a Purposeful Life, consider Mother Teresa, whom I have always admired. Although physically she was a short, thin woman her moral authority was immense. She had world leaders 'eating out of her hand'.

It is said that when Mother Teresa died all her worldly possessions were put in the bucket she used for washing. The Sisters met to discuss what they should do with her leather sandals. One Sister suggested that the sandals should be sprayed with gold paint and put on display in a glass cabinet inside the entrance of the main hospice building in Calcutta. This proposal started to gain approval until another Sister asked, 'What would Mother have wanted to do with her sandals?'

1. Uniqueness

2. Energisers/
De-energisers

3. Key strengths and
talents

4. Main beliefs and
values

5. Identity/Who I wish
to become

6. Spiritual connections

7. My Purposeful
Life is…

The answer from all the Sisters was swift and unanimous, 'Give them to the poor.'

Why did they know this? Because Mother Teresa, in spite of her occasional doubts and lack of self belief, was aligned or 'in flow' throughout her Logical Levels from her personal vision (Spiritual) to her sandals and other belongings (Environment). Furthermore, she had shared her purpose in life with her colleagues. Mother Teresa did not need a mass of personal possessions to fulfil her unique purpose in life. Furthermore, this 'calling' or vocation did not remain a dream; she took action, one step at a time.

If I had not picked up the first person [from the roadside] I would not have picked up the other 42,000.

Mother Teresa of Calcutta

We have covered a lot of ground on our journey so far. So it might be a beneficial use of time to summarise your own Purposeful Life. I suggest you summarise your thoughts in each of the clouds on pages 40–41.

Mottos, slogans and mantras

Can you use the material from the clouds to sum up your purpose in one motto, slogan, phrase or mantra? Alternatively, you might like to represent your Purposeful Life as a piece of art or create an object or choose a symbol. One business friend has a bracelet in the form of a mobius ring with the essence of who she wishes to become inscribed on the 'inside'.

My contributors shared lots of sayings which help them, or which sum up their purpose. Which ones resonate with you?

The key practice is gratitude for the amazing gift of my life, moment by moment and allowing ourselves to love ourselves.

Time spent 'reflecting' or 'being' is not rewarded. The siren voices ask us to 'do things'. How can we quieten except by silencing the siren voices?

Have new experiences – take up a new hobby, meet new people, challenge yourself...

You have to learn to forgive yourself. On days when I don't achieve much or I get panicked about time passing, I often think I have to forgive myself for going slowly or making mistakes.

When eventually I sit on the porch in that rocking chair, I want to be able to say: 'I am glad I did that' rather than 'I wish I'd done that'.

Know yourself and learn how to say 'no'.

Seek out situations or people that cause laughter.

Allow yourself to be playful again, since it is your very nature – follow your laughing thoughts!

'Make every moment count' is useful – make sure it's spent doing something you enjoy and that you feel is important – it doesn't matter what others think!

Don't waste time on regrets.

Reviewing our environment and behaviour

So far, using our 'inside-out' approach, we have focused on going inside ourselves and exploring the elements of a Purposeful Life deep within our core. However, our ability to live out our Purposeful Life day by day is influenced by the environment we find ourselves in. In the last part of the mapping journey, I therefore invite you to focus on the world around you, and how your current environment and behaviour help or hinder your Purposeful Life.

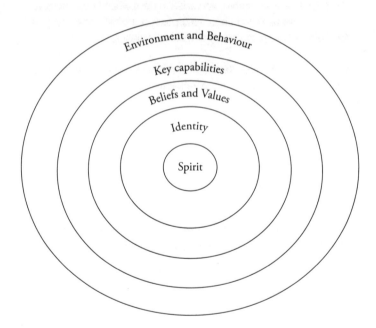

Environment and Behaviour

Key capabilities

Beliefs and Values

Identity

Spirit

Much of our current behaviour, and many of the things and people around us, will support us as we travel along our own personal pathway. Some adjustments, however, are likely to be necessary.

Look again at what you have written in the clouds as you think about the following topics. Which of the aspects below are already in place to support you on your journey, and which ones might need to be adjusted in order to open up your pathway?

As you do this, perhaps it is worth remembering the story about Mother Teresa and the saying that highly effective people travel lightly.

Behaviour	Proposed actions
Skills to let go of	
Knowledge and skills to develop	
Friends and acquaintances to let go of	
New friends and networks to develop	
Habits to change	
Qualifications to obtain	
Coaching and other support systems to develop	
Other	

Environment	Proposed actions
Financial requirements	
Physical location(s)	
IT and other equipment	
Other	

By this stage in the book you are, hopefully, getting a clearer sense of what your own Purposeful Life looks like. The obvious next step is to create an action plan.

Action plans are great, but often get left on the shelf, or, like New Year's resolutions, are followed for a bit until the challenges of everyday life get in the way.

Part 2 of this book shows you how to rebalance your time between being and doing, time with self and time with others, how to create an effective action plan by overcoming personal barriers to change, and how to sustain your Purposeful Life into the future.

Part 2

Part 2

8 Journeying with your map towards a Purposeful Life

Imagine yourself at the end of August. The summer is nearly over. Where have the first 8 months of the year gone? Time seems to fly by. Not that long ago I overheard a 22 year-old use the words, 'It's scary', when referring to how quickly the last 12 months had passed.

Having a map of a Purposeful Life is great, but how do we enact it? Why bother? Because life's too short to waste in not living in line with our purpose. As one of my contributors said:

> Time is our only fixed and finite resource. We can find ways to make water where there is not enough and food where it is scarce – science can be applied to find a solution to all resource issues (assuming someone is prepared to foot the bill) but not that of time. We will never have more than 24 hours a day and we cannot make an hour last longer than the 60 minutes that it is and always has been – not on this planet anyway.

Part 1 of this book is about understanding the aspects that make each one of us unique and the other key components of our Purposeful Lives. We can use this information to create our own personal pathway. Now is the opportunity to turn this into action. In the end, our focus will need to be on how we spend our time more intentionally (in order to resolve our first issue with time flying by!), but we now know that this action needs to be informed by having a clear understanding of our deeper purpose.

Our uniqueness is lived out in what we are, and in what we do. Most of us have a preference for either focusing inwards (who we are) or focusing outwards (what we do). To reclaim time and live a more Purposeful Life we need to look at our balance between the two – the aim is not necessarily to balance inward and outward (it's not a see-saw) but to understand how who we are influences what we do, and how what we do can, if we spend time reflecting, deepen our understanding of who we are. Being true to yourself is key.

The key elements of our unique gifts and talents, energising values and beliefs, and a sense of our own identity need to inform our actions. These will help us to use our time more intentionally. The second part of this book therefore moves outward from our core purpose to rebalance our activities in order to live a Purposeful Life.

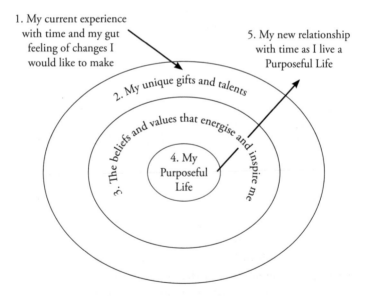

1. My current experience with time and my gut feeling of changes I would like to make

5. My new relationship with time as I live a Purposeful Life

2. My unique gifts and talents

3. The beliefs and values that energise and inspire me

4. My Purposeful Life

What does living purposefully mean for you?

Consider using these boxes to tease out how your purpose, your identity and your values and beliefs, expressed through your unique talents, could help you to see what living purposefully might look like for you.

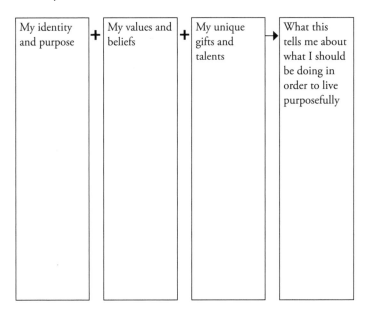

A portrait of living purposefully

Based on the words of many of my contributors, here is a portrait of what it's like to live purposefully:

I am in balance. It starts with a good night's sleep. I get up with energy and a sense of positive momentum. I feel good about life in the present moment. I invest my mind, heart, soul and spirit into the work for that day. I focus on the quality of my relationships and release a flow of love.

I am fully engaged with what I am doing and aligned at every level. There is a sense of being in rhythm with something. I can switch with ease between the different levels and types of interaction that the day brings – including at home.

I feel happier and fulfilled. I feel good – mentally, physically, emotionally and spiritually. I have a feeling of completion, as if the air were filling up my lungs at their fullest. I feel at peace with who I am and I am working with using the gifts and talents that I have, rather than wasting my time worrying about trying to be something else or regretting not being someone else.

When I am active in what I want to do, I sense that time is my ally; it flows in the action of what I do, and flows in harmony. On such days, time is just the container that provides a humane context for the day. Without time there would not be the boundaries or structures that allow for the rhythms of human life and experience, (for example, the feeling of tired satisfaction, or appreciation of coming to a restful point after achievement).

When I am at one with the universe, I am not thinking about time at all. I do not 'make use of time' in a utilitarian sense – I am part of time and time is only a man-made frame around us all. I am connected to my source, and I am aware of my priorities.

My research contributors reported that when they were living purposefully they felt a sense of alignment, of being in contact with something steadying, of being on track. The feelings associated with being in this alignment included joy, peace, a sense of time not mattering, satisfaction, being in control. How do they know when they are living purposefully? Some have a sense of being totally absorbed and 'in the moment', others feel a sense of freedom, and for some it's about having time for reflection or down-time:

When I am in the moment, I become calm and can feel a deep sense of oneness which comes from deep inside.

When I'm making a difference to someone (including myself), I'm being fully present to whoever is with me, or my surroundings.

When I'm reliving an event – time is not escaping but being used well.

When I am one with the task, one with the universe.

When I am connected to my source, I am aware of my priorities.

When I follow my inner promptings and trust my inner voice.

When I can choose to be where I am and do what I want to do.

When I have playtime: new ideas, original thoughts and language, great laughter.

When I do something really special, something new that I've never done before.

When I spend time with the family.

When I have times of stillness and quiet.

When I don't have to fill every hour or every day with some meaningful task or activity.

Adopting a purposeful mindset

My research contributors offered a wealth of ideas and activities to help keep a purposeful mindset. Before you start planning and committing to the specific changes you want to make in your life, you might like to look at these and see if some of them are helpful.

Let go of unhelpful mindsets

List the messages about time that you were given as a child. Notice how you react when you have nothing to do. Decide which messages to let go of.

Plan for what you want in life

Give yourself the gift of time to plan and move towards your dreams. If you do not take the time to think and plan, life will just happen and you may wake up one day with regrets.

Focus on what is important

Work out what's most important beforehand, and make sure it happens. Choose when to allow distractions/diversions and when to shut them out.

Review your purpose

Focus on your purpose, rather than on all the things you haven't managed to get done. Use it to evaluate whether what you're doing is 'on track'.

Connect to your inner source

Do not fill every second of the day; take moments for inner reflection and ask questions such as:

- What is really important for you now?
- What are you here for, what is your mission?

The Divine within

If you believe that the Divine is within you, how might this help to change your outlook on your purpose and how you spend your time?

Engaged, involved, meaningful

In his book, *Learned Optimism*, Martin Seligman describes the three 'essential oils' or 'pathways' of life:

1. Be emotionally engaged – 'a pleasant life'.
2. Be fully connected with both your internal and external activities (thinking, feeling and doing) – 'an engaged life'.
3. Be fully and actively involved in your life through personal meaning and spirituality (not necessarily religious but purposeful) – 'a meaningful life'.

Be prepared to leave undone

From the *Rule of Life* of the Companions of Brother Lawrence:
- Deliberately choose what things you will leave undone or postpone.
- Instead of being oppressed by a clutter of unfinished jobs, think out your priorities under God.
- Accept, without guilt or resentment, the fact that much you had thought you ought to do, you must leave.

Practise the presence of the Divine

Trust your inner voice – listen hard to what you feel you're supposed to do next.

Contact something greater than you

Rest each day in the presence of God or the universe. Anchor your life in what St. Paul referred to as 'the peace that passes all understanding'. No matter what the day brings, believe you will be able to access the resources necessary to live well within it.

Quotations for adopting a purposeful mindset

Yesterday is a memory, tomorrow is a mystery and today is a gift, which is why it is called the present.
Anon

Time is life. If you love life, do not squander time for it is the stuff of which life is made.
Benjamin Franklin

Live your life and forget your age.
Norman Vincent Peale

Your time is limited, so don't waste it living someone else's life. Don't be trapped by dogma – which is living with the results of someone else's thinking. Don't let the noise of other's opinions drown out your own inner voice. And most important, have the courage to follow your heart and intuition. They somehow already know what you truly want to become. Everything else is secondary…. You've got to find out what you love…. The only way to be truly satisfied is to do what you believe is great work. And the only way to do great work is to love what you do. If you haven't found it yet keep looking. Don't settle. As with all matters of the heart, you'll know when you have found it. And, like any great relationship, it just gets better and better as the years roll on. So keep looking till you find it.
Steve Jobs

9 The importance of being

What is interesting about the way my research contributors described living purposefully, is that it is only partly about *doing*. Many people feel that there is a conflict between experiences that help them to feel in flow, and what society values as an effective use of time. Is 'making the most of time' when we are most productive and getting lots of stuff done *or* is it when we are doing what we really value with people we really value? In the twenty-first century's hurry culture the former often gets greater emphasis than the latter.

Looking back over my life I can see that I was conditioned as a child into believing that I had to work hard in order to get on. It's clear that I am not alone in being continually busy and 'doing things'. It is as though our whole society has been enticed to step onto a giant hamster wheel called 'busy-ness', where it has become uncomfortable to raise questions such as: 'Where is this leading me?' 'What's all this in aid of?' 'What am I on this planet for?'

The being–doing loop

There is a strong relationship between who I am (my being, my character) and what I do (my personality). I believe that unless we have a strong character and core around our 'being' the whole edifice called 'doing' is liable to collapse when times get really tough, e.g. in situations where we ask questions like: 'Who am I now that I am redundant/divorced/the children have left home?'

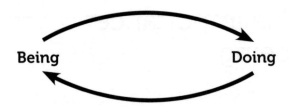

Many self help books and training courses are skills based and focus on doing. Much rarer are books or courses that focus on character – on building integrity, honesty, personal trustworthiness, clarifying our uniqueness and who we wish to become.

Most people spend the majority of their time 'doing', as this is what most of us have been rewarded for from our school days right through our career. We therefore give lower priority to spending time reflecting, recharging our batteries, working on our character and other aspects of our 'being'.

Doing is important; but to live a Purposeful Life we need to balance our doing with being – and that was reinforced by many of my contributors.

Traditional personal development programmes have action plans, and there is a feeling that you need to 'do' stuff in order to change. My own reflections and the responses from my research suggest that rather, we need to adjust the balance between the various aspects of our lives, and for many of us, that means giving more time to being activities, so that we can do our doing more intentionally.

Architect Frank Lloyd Wright told how a lecture he received at the age of nine helped set his philosophy of life.

An uncle, a stolid, no-nonsense type, had taken him for a long walk across a snow-covered field. At the far side, his uncle told him to look back at their two sets of tracks. 'See my boy,' he said, 'how your footprints go aimlessly back and forth from those trees, to the cattle, back to the fence and then over there to where you were throwing sticks? But notice how my path comes straight across, directly to my goal. You should never forget this lesson.'

'And I never did,' Wright said. 'I determined right then not to miss most things in life, as my uncle had.'

What is important to you in order to feel purposeful – when you are organising and planning, or when you are simply receiving and experiencing time?

Experiencing/		Organising/
receiving		planning
BEING		DOING

Living purposefully through being

Some people don't have an over-arching need to fill every hour or every day with some meaningful task or activity in order to feel they are living a Purposeful Life. Making progress or moving towards completing a task is satisfying and gives a sense of well being, but time spent with family and times of stillness and quiet are also crucial in restoring the soul even though there is no measurable way of identifying what has been accomplished.

It's too easy to lose the real you when life continually runs at a fast pace. For many people, living a Purposeful Life means taking time out and slowing down. On good days they finish one thought or action before the next one appears. Equally energising is 'doing nothing well', e.g. choosing to have a 'pyjama day' spent watching a few really good films with the family.

Taking time out – doing something different – gives the space to grow and find oneself again, even to find a new part of the self. Although we may feel purposeful when we are ticking things off a list, the times we feel we are 'making the most of our time' are when we are making a difference to someone (including ourselves) by doing very little but being fully present to whoever is with us, or to our surroundings. Going for a really nice walk, alone or with someone we want to be with, is making the most of our time.

When people living purposefully do engage in something that holds their attention, most other things become of secondary importance. Don't bother calling them for meals, breaks, or whatever – when they are engaged it can be difficult to distract them. They are in 'flow' (as described by Mihály Csikszentmihalyi in his book *Flow*); they do what they are doing, be it work or anything else, effortlessly yet efficiently. It's when they are absorbed by what they are doing (even if it's listening to a CD); being in flow feels balanced, relaxed yet animating.

Many of our contributors talked about being in touch with their Purposeful Life as being fully in the present moment. 'When we feel guilt, regret, resentment, grievance, sadness, bitterness, we know we are in the past and need to shift attention deeply back into the present. When we feel fear, unease, anxiety, tension, stress, worry, we know we are in the future and need to shift attention deeply into the present.' Things happen in flow when we are in the mood for them to happen, bringing a sense of accomplishment without effort, a sense of some real time spent in relaxation.

They feel that if they can pay full attention to what they are doing or who they are with, then – if they're lucky – they can get the hands of the clock to hesitate, ever so slightly. It's more of a happy surprise. The slowing down brings about a different state of being; it's not about doing, it is about being no matter what they are doing. If they start multi-tasking again, if they try to think, listen, talk, read and write at the same time, it's lost. Time speeds up.

Reflection, mindfulness, prayer or meditation can help to achieve this. When we reflect, we are present in the moment and time is not so much of an issue. Meditating first thing in the morning can help the day go smoothly so that everything that needs to get done in that day is done without any interruptions or challenges. The internalising is reflected in the outer world.

And as one contributor put it, there are moments when life feels complete in itself:

> Time slowed down in all the days and nights I spent in places I travelled to – I lived so slowly in the high mountains, the countryside of my homeland, the deserts of the Middle East, the cities of India, the Himalayan villages…. There you are confronted with physical toil and you discover how strong is solidarity and how good it is to do work with others, for others. True connection to another human being, to the soul of nature: that's the place where time is meaningful and I can accept it, going beyond it.

Quotations to help being

The most wasted day of all is that during which we have not laughed.
Sebastian R. N. Chamfort

Not even the wisest nor richest man can make time shorter or longer for even one second.
Ivo Andric

Man who treats life like a race gets to the end very quickly!
Confucius

To see a world in a grain of sand
And a heaven in a wild flower,
Hold infinity in the palm of your hand
And eternity in an hour.
'Auguries of Innocence', William Blake

Until you value yourself, you will not value your time. Until you value
your time, you will not do anything with it.
M. Scott Peck

People like you and I, though mortal of course like everyone else, do
not grow old no matter how long we live. We never cease to stand like
curious children before the great mystery into which we were born.
Albert Einstein

Everything that has a beginning has an ending. Make your peace
with that and all will be well.
Buddhist saying

We are supposed to be human beings but many of us spend our lives
as human *doings*. Maybe we were told on more than one occasion
'Don't just stand there, do something!'

Most of us need to encourage ourselves to be more and do less. Perhaps
we should tell ourselves 'Don't just do something, stand there.'

What is this life if, full of care,
We have no time to stop and stare.
'Leisure', William Henry Davies

Let's become human becomings

The next chapter has lots of ideas from our contributors about how
to develop your being, realising the truth in 'less is more' and 'work
smarter, not harder'.

10 Anchoring your being

Our being is the anchor which is going to ground our purposeful doing; that is what makes it robust, particularly in the face of difficulties. My contributors gave me lots of ideas about how to anchor being, and one of the most crucial was the art of being in the present moment.

Most of us spend our time living in a mixture of the past and the future. We see the world through the filters of our past experiences or our hopes and fears about the future, and we spend very little time actually noticing what's really happening, free from opinions, judgements, assumptions or fears. For example, right now, just raise your eyes from this page and look over the top of the book/screen at whatever's behind it. What do you see? Keep looking at it while you count to 10.

What other thoughts, opinions, judgements came into your mind during those 10 seconds? Most of us (including the author!) find it virtually impossible to keep our minds on what's actually in front of us, to really *see* what we're looking at, to be present in this moment in time.

Being in the moment

Here are some ideas and activities from my contributors, for practising mindfulness, or being in the moment and for being still.

Live more in the moment

- Stop your mind wandering to future events.
- Make the most of occasions such as birthdays.

Catch yourself in the moment

- Remember to notice what's going on for you, for others, for the world.
- Physically slow down and breathe...
- Zoom out and see yourself from a distance.

Celebrate

Stop and think about what is going right, right now and celebrate.

Look out of the window at nature

- Get yourself a drink and pause for a minute or two to look out of a window.
- See the changes that each season brings.

Enjoy all the small things

- The first snowdrop.
- A glimpse of sunshine on a rainy day.
- Hearing a beautiful piece of music or an interesting idea on the radio.

Be curious

Stop and look at familiar things, e.g. a leaf or a snail, through the curious eyes of a child or of a Leonardo da Vinci.

Wholeheartedly do what you are doing

- When you eat, put your whole attention to the eating without judgement or bias.

- When you breathe, put your whole attention to breathing without judgement or bias.
- When you walk, put your whole attention to walking without judgement or bias.

Practice awareness

Say 'I am aware of…' over and over as you become aware of different things, e.g. what you are seeing, what you are feeling, how you are responding, what you are hearing, what you are thinking and so on.

Focus on today

Emulate John Ruskin, the nineteenth-century art critic and social thinker, who had a stone on his desk bearing the word 'Today'.

Break your thought patterns

Liberate yourself, discover yourself. Who are you? You are not what you think you are, but what you think. Overcome false identities. Your actions are connected to what you think.

Mindfulness of breath

Become conscious of your bodily sensations. Attend closely to the breath stream going in and out of the nostrils or mouth. Calmly notice the sensation and any change of sensation, without analysis. Observe any thoughts as 'just thoughts' without judgement. Bring your attention back to the breath going in and out. Observe feelings as 'just feelings'; don't dwell on them.

Body scan – extending mindfulness

Move your attention from one part of your body to another. Become more aware of yourself in the moment and in a non-judgemental, accepting way; a kind of 'falling awake'. This can be guided by listening to a CD or by using a learned sequence.

Still the mind

Focus on your breathing:
1. Sit comfortably and close your eyes.
2. Breathe in through your nose.
3. Breathe out though your mouth.
4. Repeat 10 times.

Infinite time, infinite space

Practice meditation. In one moment, there is infinite time, infinite space.

Travelling

- Some of us spend a large chunk of the week travelling. How do you optimise this time?
- What can you do to slow yourself down?
- How can you put the past and the future to one side and bring yourself totally into the present?
- Two of the great things about meditation are that you can do it without a doctor's prescription and it is portable! So if you are travelling by train or on a bus how about using 10 minutes of your journey time in meditation?

Attentiveness

Have you ever been with someone who, even in a crowded room, focused on you 100% as if you were the only other person on this planet? Even some very busy or famous people seem to be able to put their own life story aside to focus solely on another person. This level of attentiveness, in my opinion, is one of the most precious things you can give to other people. How about practising this?

A useful anagram

The words 'listen' and 'silent' are composed of the same letters. Perhaps there is a message here!

Finding balance

Balance is the state of the present – the here and now.
If you are balanced in the present, you are living
in eternity. When the intellect is stable there is
no past, no future, only present.

B K S Iyengar

The mind tends to focus on either the worries and anxieties of the future or on the memories, regrets and guilt of the past. Eckhart Tolle, in his book, *A New Earth*, refers to the 'mode of having' which exists only in time – past, present and future, and the 'mode of being' which exists in the here and now.

Being still

Make time for yourself

No one else will, and you will go mad if you don't! Refresh and recharge, free from the tyranny of the immediate, day-to-day tasks and pressures. Be alone, in a favourite setting or location. That way you can catch the still, quiet voice of God.

Be still at the beginning of the day

Note down the people, events and concerns which whirl through your head. Come back within yourself, enter more fully into the present moment.

Spend time in prayer and silence

- Be still, morning and evening – sit (or kneel) in silence.
- After lunch spend a further 30 minutes sitting down being quiet.

Trust the process

- Take time to pray or meditate.
- Trust that God or the universe will help you make good use of your time.

Share silence with others

Share 20 minutes silence one early evening a week with a small group.

Meditate on a mantra

For example: 'I am a soul, a peaceful, loving soul. Whatever is happening is happening for the best. I have enough, I do enough and I am enough.'

Create a quiet room/space

Create a place not of work or doing, but a place of rest and being; carpeted, with one or two small lounge chairs and a spiritual picture to hang on one of the walls.

Stillness in stressful moments

Stop everything, and concentrate on your breathing using the ancient Jesus Prayer: 'Lord Jesus Christ, Son of God,' – during the in breath – 'have mercy on me a sinner' – during the out breath. The breathing should be deep and steady.

The inner tortoise or the inner child

As a young boy I had a pet tortoise. I was fascinated by it and by other animals that moved very slowly and yet, in relation to their size, could soon move across a large area. At the very beginning of this project I thought of using 'Bring out the Inner Tortoise' as the book title or as a chapter title.

What practical tips on time are associated with this idea?

Quotations for being in the moment and being still

There are moments when time suddenly stops and becomes eternal.
F. Dostoyevsky

There is more to life than increasing its speed.
Gandhi

The subconscious is ceaselessly murmuring, and it is by listening to these murmurs that one hears the truth.
Gaston Bachelard

Blessed are those who see beautiful things in humble places where others see nothing.
Camille Pissarro

It is a very good plan every now and then to go away and have a little relaxation. When you come back to the work your judgement will be surer, since to remain constantly at work will cause you to lose the power of judgement.
Leonardo da Vinci

Lead the life that will make you kindly and friendly to everyone about you, and you will be surprised what a happy life you will lead.
Charles M. Schwab

You have the opportunity to choose what your children's parents will be.
Richard Fox

11 Building being into your daily life

Now that you have read about the advantages of being in the present moment and being still, the challenge is to build space for that into your daily life. Here are some practical ideas from my contributors. Their tips fall into five main sections; start where you like:

• Manage your daily rhythm
• Break free from the automatic need to DO
• Be physically active
• Build relationships
• Find a new attitude to life and time.

I hope you will find that these ideas will start to buy you time to be in the moment, to enjoy being where you are. I kick off with some short 'off the peg' tips and at the end of this chapter I have included some longer, more powerful exercises.

Manage your daily rhythm

Use different approaches for work and leisure times

• How about organising leisure time completely differently from how you organise work time?

Work	Leisure
To-do list	Be and Do
Watch the clock	Ignore the clock
Wear a watch	Put your watch in a drawer
Smartphone on	Smartphone off

Balance your energy

- Refocus where you are spending your energy to ensure you have no regrets later.
- Balance the energy you spend on work and the energy you spend on family and friends.

Balance your life

- A good night's sleep gives energy and a sense of positive momentum.
- Spend time in prayer, exercise, and cooking and eating wholesome food.
- Invest your mind, heart and soul into your work for that day.
- Focus on the quality of your relationships – with your children, your partner, those you encounter during the day.

Live in daytime compartments

- Start the day by focusing on the two or three most critical things you need to achieve in the day.
- Make sure you do these well.
- Celebrate their achievement at the end of the day.

Keep your sanity!

- Count to ten before you reply to an awkward question. This gives you time to assess what is being asked and has a calming effect if you have been angered.
- Take a deep breath.
- Relax and stare into space, lose yourself in time.
- Allow time in the day for unforeseen occurrences.
- Have a long soak in the bath.
- Switch off your mobile phone.
- Take time for yourself, say to yourself that you deserve it and don't feel guilty about doing this.

Take a break

- Take an occasional break away from the workplace – a chance to pause and take a breath.
- Travel out to visit clients in their premises.
- Pull off on the journey and take a break. Take this time to reflect and connect to your priorities in life (read the Bible, pray…).

Adjust your internal/psychological clock

Set an internal dial or hands on a clock. Slow it down when you are enjoying things and speed it up if there is something you want to get over very quickly.

Chill out while waiting

- Don't get frustrated by meetings not starting on time or by delays in travelling.
- Carry a set of cards or a notebook to write your thoughts down in as you wait.

Take a cat nap

And then review your to-do list. You will find there are things you can drop or defer, making you feel better.

Take a bath, not a shower

Relax in a bath for 25 minutes. Feel the tension ease between your shoulders; sense things that were whirling around in your head fall into place without any apparent assistance from you.

Notice your learning each day

Write down your learning each day – what you have noticed, what has surprised you, what has been confirmed again. Even on days when you feel you haven't achieved much, there is still learning.

Use a trigger

When you think time is running away use a trigger, e.g. Simon and Garfunkel's '59th Street Bridge Song', with the words:

> Slow down, you move too fast
> You've got to make the morning last.

Calm down at the end of the day

- Take a glass of something you like.
- Read something that is not directly related to your work.
- Read something that allows you to think about the bigger picture – years and decades.

Do something you enjoy

- Read for pleasure.
- Immerse yourself in playing an instrument.

Use the rhythm of poetry

Make poems or other beautiful language part of your normal waking consciousness. If poems or prayers are memorised, they can travel with you as you walk.

Being snowed in

The days of being snowed up seemed longer than other days.
Why should that be?

- Normal daily work routine disrupted?
- You cannot go where you planned to go?
- You have nothing to do because nothing was planned?

How can you replicate this experience during the rest of the year?
Who are you when there's nothing to do, nowhere to be, or no one to meet?

Break free from the automatic need to do

Take a day of rest and be thankful

- Write down the things you're mentally going to 'leave behind' for the day.
- Put the list, your watch and phone in a drawer.
- Turn off the computer and TV.
- Turn to your spouse, child, parent or friend and just talk, and listen.
- Pick up a book. Take some time to be thankful – alone or in community.

Reflect on the past week

- Every week or so, look back over the past week and write about the things you have done and your thoughts about them.
- Recognise the cyclical nature of many things and slow down your perspective of time.

Take regular longer breaks

From time to time (weekly, monthly, annually) take a period of longer rest. Resting brings joy, thankfulness and freedom to enjoy all that is good about life.

Have a rule of life

For example:
- Take a twice yearly or annual retreat (to reflect and review or just be).
- Take regular holidays.
- Continue to study.
- Travel.

Keep the horizons of life open so that the inner-being can be expressed and the inner-child kept vibrant.

Be physically active

Walking

Go for a long hike in the countryside. Notice in detail what's around you – stop to look more closely at trees, flowers, birds.

Exercise and fluids

Exercise and drink lots of water. This gives you energy to enjoy the day.

Do repetitive exercise

For example, swimming. Free up your mind to be available to anything God and/or the universe might want to say.

Do facial exercises

- Relax facial muscles at regular intervals.
- Close your eyes and allow your whole face to sink towards the earth.
- Then open your eyes as wide as possible and smile widely.

Make a weekly commitment to relaxing exercise

Factor into your normal week a commitment to relax, e.g. with a hobby or exercise such as Pilates, Tai Chi, yoga, or meditation.

Do yoga

Focus on the importance of using energy wisely and not dissipating it through fruitless anxiety about the past and future. Focus on the 'here and now'; this will channel your energy more effectively so you can achieve more, with greater peace of mind.

Do body work

Use body work (e.g. yoga, Tai Chi, Qi Gong etc) to help you meditate and get grounded once more when a thought messes things up.

Build relationships

Make people happy

- Make the most of whatever time you have with the people that matter to you.
- Make yourself and others happy, as far as you are able.
- Spend time working out what happiness means for you.
- Happiness is probably a by-product of other things.

'Waste time' with people

Be patient with whatever is important for them.

Be with animals, children, gardens, music, dreams and myths

- Let children take the lead. Lose yourself. Join in their world.
- Do the same when you are sitting stroking a cat or a dog.
- Let music, dreams and myths engage your unconscious and simultaneously reference the horizontal and vertical elements of consciousness.

Make time for self, spouse and family

At least once a day.

Help others and stretch yourself

Spend time on things that help others and stretch you to grow as a person. This will be time you can savour for a long time to come.

Help others

Think of one thing you could do to help a friend, family member or colleague right now – and go do it.

Have quality conversations with your partner

Plan an undisturbed conversation twice a month (no mobile, doorbell, kids, etc.). One of you talks, uninterrupted, for 15 minutes about how things are. How am I doing? How do I feel our relationship is going? How are things for me? The other person may not speak or interfere during this period. Then swap roles.

Build new attitudes and beliefs about time

In order to change our everyday life, we need to dig down and adjust some of our attitudes and beliefs. This is challenging! But my contributors said that these ideas and practices helped them to find the space to let new behaviours come in. You might like to try out a few of them for a few weeks, to see how they help you re-balance your relationship with time.

Keep a thankful diary or a gratitude journal

I heard a story recently of a man who was totally demotivated at work. He felt he was trapped in his current job and that it was unrealistic for him to look elsewhere for another job. He decided to write a gratitude journal. Every evening he would record an event from the day for which he was thankful, no matter how small that event was. After some months his colleagues and friends noticed a significant improvement in his mood and general demeanour. Within one year he was promoted into a more worthwhile job. Why not try this for yourself? Without waiting until you are feeling depressed!

Sleep on it

Scientists are now able to confirm what the human race has known intuitively for thousands of years – it helps to sleep on it. Delay a decision, particularly if the issues are complicated. Ask your other than conscious mind to work on the problem whilst you are asleep or enjoying an outing with a friend. A better decision is likely to emerge than one taken on the spur of the moment.

Learn from the Chinese

How might the Five Elements, or the dynamic relationship between Yin and Yang or the principles of Feng Shui help us to slow down the passing of time?

Outer and inner space

Physical locations can affect our perceptions of time. There is a Buddhist saying: 'If you want to experience equanimity you need to put yourself in a vast space. In the vastness equanimity is given to you.'

For me there's a difference between sitting quietly in a cathedral and arriving at a busy mainline station. Being in a room with a high ceiling can slow me down. I book such a room when I want some private study/retreat time, for example when I was writing this book.

What location(s) might you choose to slow down the passing of time?

Slow down the fast bits

Jackie Stewart, multiple World Champion racing driver said that the right mental technique to get round a corner or a sequence of track as quickly as possible was to slow it down in the mind as much as possible. It's a good technique, although not directly applicable to road driving!

In what situations might this be useful to you?

Looking at things differently

Some years ago I worked with George, who has since become a close friend. One of the things that amazed me about George was that he worked long hours but always seemed sharp and full of energy. On one occasion he told me that when he got home from work he would cook the evening meal for his wife and four children, clear away all the dishes and then change the cat litter tray. I asked him if he resented doing this. He replied 'No, I could resent having to do this but I love my wife and children and I choose to do it as an act of love. On one level the task remains the same. At another level it is transformed from a chore to a pleasure because of my attitude towards it.'

What task do you do on a regular basis that could be transformed by changing your mental perception towards it?

In time or through time

Here's a fun exercise to do with a group.

Stand in a circle, far enough apart that you don't touch each other when you move your arms about.

Explain that this exercise is about your personal perceptions of your past, your present and your future. There are no right or wrong answers, or better than/worse than answers.

1.Your own past
(a) Shut your eyes and without thinking point to your past.
(b) Whilst keeping your arms and hands still, open your eyes and look around the room. Notice the similarities and differences between where you and others are pointing. Some differences will be quite subtle, others more obvious.

2. Your present
(a) Now come into the present moment. Shut your eyes again and, without thinking about it, point to your present.
(b) Repeat 1 (b) above.

3. Your future

Repeat 1(a) and (b) above for your own future and then pair up with someone whose internal maps of time seem to be different from yours. Discuss how these differences manifest in, for example:

(a) The detail with which you can recall your past.

(b) Your attitudes to deadlines, punctuality, urgency, time management.

(c) Detailed plans for the future?

Shifting our focus

The following idea came from a BBC Radio 4 'Thought for the Day' on 21 January 2010. The speaker from the Iona Community in Scotland invited the listener to focus on being rather than doing, and giving rather than possessing.

He suggested that the fear of dying is based on the loss of what we have – our possessions and/or our egos.

Are there some shifts you could make to your lifestyle to ease the pressure of time?

Choose a new attitude to life and time

One of my contributors sent me the following:

Think of time as the air you take in and breathe out, think of time as that constant flow of life, running gently along with you, as the rhythm of your actions. If you move gently time will move in the same way. Remember time is just a thought away, you can flow with it, and you can make time flow with you. You are the master of time, you are the conqueror of it, you tame it at your will, you make it your ally!! Time never helps when you rush it!!

Imagine time saying 'Think of me as a gentle breeze caressing your moves. Think of me as the companion that holds your hand to enjoy the moment. Think of me as if I did not exist, because in fact I do not! I am only in your mind! Master that thought, be creative, and you will master me!'

Making a being plan

Get your notebook and write down your answers to the following questions:

• What being activities do you want to build into the way you spend your time?

• What actions can you take on these within the next few days/ weeks?

• Who will you need to tell, so that they understand what you're doing and why?

• How will you know when it feels right?

12 Using being to make your doing much more effective

Living purposefully shows itself in what we do and how we do it in the light of what we have found out about our purpose, values, beliefs and unique talents/contribution. Although for some people a Purposeful Life can be lived out by enacting the being activities we have been exploring, many of us feel that we live out a Purposeful Life by actively doing, which means getting things done, by getting good feedback about what we have done and how it has been valued by others.

For many of my contributors, a good day starts with good intent and a good plan. They may have a long to-do list of items but they know where they have to go. They are enthusiastically doing what they love to do. They're usually doing things that can be easily quantified – quite often they are visible and/or countable. Whilst they may have no control over other people's interactions with them, they know the territory and the route they're traversing. It's a joyous journey.

For some people, effective doing is about being in personal control of the situation they find themselves in, choosing where they are and what they do. Then they are not distracted or interrupted; they are focussed on achieving the few important tasks for the day rather than being jerked around by 'noise'. They can make progress on their own agenda rather than reacting to the whims of others. For others what matters is to be proactive, to be moving forward rather than maintaining the status quo; some original thought, or practical output must occur. Emptying the in-tray is not enough.

Many of my research contributors confirmed the feeling that doing something meaningful happens when they are aligned with their purpose. Sometimes they have worked hard to define their purpose; sometimes they listen to their inner promptings in the moment; they trust their inner voice, listening hard to determine what they're supposed to do next.

For some people, the interface between being and doing is less clearly defined – doing can mean being with and/or working for others, with people that they feel comfortable and relaxed with, able to be themselves completely, or playing and/or doing something new. In 'playtime' all sorts of things arise freshly from experience: new ideas, original thoughts and language, laughter, a stream of consciousness showing more realities and possibilities. It's the kind of magical fireworks that leads to great things. Special days are when they have done something new that they have never done before.

Activities for using your doing time more intentionally

'To achieve great things, two things are needed, a plan, and not quite enough time.'

Leonard Bernstein

Once you've got a sense of living purposefully and how you want to be, you can trawl the time management books for tips on how to plan the use of your time. In addition, here are some tips from my contributors to help you use your doing time more effectively. I suggest you mark one or two that you might find particularly useful.

Set your intent for the day

Decide on the quality of the relationship you want with the people you are meeting, or identify an opportunity to use one or more of your core talents and strengths.

Take time to plan

Prioritise planning each day and write a journal each evening, to plan for time conflicts and improve your emotional resilience. This will more than compensate for the time you would otherwise spend orientating and debriefing yourself.

Be prepared

Get your preparation done now so that you can have fun while others are still preparing.

An overall annual plan

Put up a yearly planning poster that allows you to see the whole year in a single glance. This will help you keep your focus and perspective on the major milestones for the next 1+ years.

Make short lists

Keep your to-do list to 10 things or less. And turn your email off for certain parts of the day, to help avoid distractions.

Turn your list into action

- Prioritise the list.
- Keep rigorously to the priorities.
- Do one task at a time until it is finished.
- Use mindmaps. If the statement ' a picture is worth a thousand words' is true for you, create a mindmap instead of a list. *The Mindmap Book* by T. Buzan is a good place to begin.

Database of ideas

If you have an idea whose time has not yet come, make a note of it in your diary 12 months ahead and forget about it until then.

Stop doing list

We are all familiar with to-do lists. How about creating, at least once a year, a 'stop doing' list?

Perhaps list

If some things on your to-do list keep not getting done, don't beat yourself up. Could they move to a 'perhaps list' or should you drop them altogether?

The Pomodoro Method

Set a kitchen timer and work for 25 minutes in a focused manner. When the timer goes off, set it for five minutes and process emails, stretch or 'play'. Every fourth session, take a longer break.

Putting off interruptions for 25 minutes doesn't take too much will power, and yet you can get a lot of quality work done in each 'pomodoro'.

Manage your interruptions

- Screen your phone calls and answer those that need a response at a more appropriate time.
- Allocate your schedule so it fits with your most productive times of the day.
- Learn to say 'no' nicely.
- Under promise and over deliver – much more satisfying for all than the other way around.

Manage your relationship with email

Acknowledge the twitchy addiction we have to checking for emails every time we can:

- Only check emails at set times of the day.
- Do you need to send it at all? And to all of the people you're copying it to?
- Could you instead walk over to talk to the person or phone them?
- Are you clear what you want by when, and what the person can do if that's not possible?
- Before pressing 'send' ask yourself: 'How would I feel if I got that email?'

Weekends free of business messages

Stop checking business messages in your emails and social media over the weekend. Graveyards are full of people who thought they were indispensable!

Overseas business trips

Always plan in an extra day before your business meeting to explore and relax in the city you are visiting.

Programme of regular change

For example, change your job or your home or your leisure interests on a regular basis. Prevent your mind from becoming used to the status quo and blanking out the unfamiliar. Receiving completely new stimuli seems to slow down time.

Find boring things to do

One of the characters in the book *Catch 22* is Dunbar. He loves shooting skeet because he hates every minute of it and time passes so slowly when he does it. He recognised that a single hour on the skeet shooting range could be worth as much as eleven-times-seventeen years.

Quotations to help doing

Time wastes our bodies and our wits, but we waste time so we are quits.
Sundial, 1746

Time and tide wait for no man.
Proverb

Many of life's failures are people who did not realise how close they were to success when they gave up.
Thomas Edison

Knowing is not enough; we must apply. Willing is not enough; we must do.
Goethe

The secret of happiness is not in doing what one likes, but in liking what one does.
James M Barrie

Wise and mature people have only as much time as they can spend. Excess free time spoils people.
Dushan Radovich

When a goal matters enough to a person, that person will find a way to accomplish what at first seemed impossible.
Nido Qubein

Opportunities multiply as they are seized.
Sun Tzu

No one made a greater mistake than he who did nothing because he thought he could only do a small thing.
Edmund Burke

Developing a doing plan

I hope the above gives you some ideas for a plan to help you use your doing time more intentionally. Use the following questions to help you identify some actions you can take now.

What small steps or private experiments could you make in the next week?

What do you need to tell others, and who do you need to tell, as you change the way you work with your purpose?

How will you know when it's going well?

---

13 Balancing your Purposeful Life – between self and others

We've looked at working from the inside out through understanding our purpose, values, beliefs and unique talents.

We've looked at balancing being and doing.

The final part of the Purposeful Life model looks at how you balance your internal and external life; time spent alone and time spent with others.

You often hear the phrase 'my private life and my business life'. Life is short enough already, so why divide it into two? You also hear the term 'work–life balance', which again I find unsatisfactory as it implies that you can only have a life when you are not working! Perhaps a better term is 'a balanced life' or simply 'a life'!

Self and others

Some people may feel that they are constantly at the beck and call of 'others' and would love to have some quality time alone to, for example, live their own life, learn a foreign language, meditate or simply be!

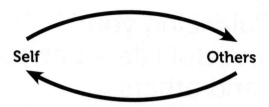

What's your present balance like between self and others? On average, where do you spend your time between self (time alone) and time spent with others?

_____

Now that you're getting very close to a complete action plan, have a look at it and think about how you need to adjust your plans for:

(a) Being versus doing

(b) Time with self versus time with others

_____

You now have a complete approach to a Purposeful Life, which will help you to use your time more intentionally. Together we have looked at most of the components of my Purposeful Life model.

We started on the outer ring of the model when we looked at our current experience with time and our gut feelings of changes we would like to make. We then entered the heart of the model to unearth our unique gifts and talents; the core beliefs and values that guide us and we mapped our own Purposeful Life. We now return to the outer ring to create a new relationship with time and decide on strategies to sustain our Purposeful Life action plan.

Inside-out approach to a Purposeful Life

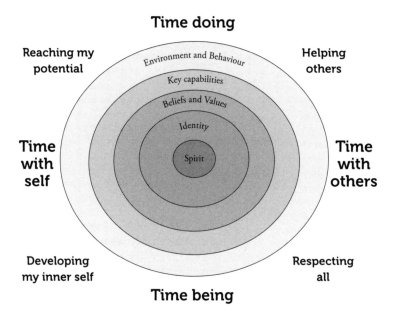

Time doing

Reaching my
potential

Helping
others

**Time
with
self**

Environment and Behaviour

Key capabilities

Beliefs and Values

Identity

Spirit

**Time
with
others**

Developing
my inner self

Respecting
all

Time being

One of the inspirations behind the above model is Marjo Lips-
Wiersma, University of Canterbury, New Zealand and her research
on holistic development.

14 Making it real – enacting your plan

Now that you have explored your Purposeful Life, I hope you are starting to come up with practical ideas for changes you can make in your life.

As I worked on the book, pulling out themes and arranging material into sections, I realised that there can be a gap between wanting to do something and actually doing it.

- What is likely to hold you back from making the changes you want to see in your own life?
- What are the current benefits of your old way of doing things, including your use of time?
- How might you retain these benefits whilst making the desired changes?
- What is likely to stop you making the changes?
- What support could you ask for from other people?

My coaching and consultancy firm, The Learning Corporation LLP, has developed a Six Step Change Process to help you map where you want to go, what stops you from taking action, and how you can overcome these barriers to change.

I decided that if I was going to invite you to work through this model, I should share my completed Six Step Process with you. Heather Brown volunteered to do the same. So in the Appendix you can find two examples of how we used the Six Step Change Process to work through the things we personally wanted to change about our own relationships with time.

We both found the process of working through the six steps useful, in helping us to notice our assumptions and the beliefs that hold them in place, and in finding the points of leverage or nudge which will enable us to spend our time differently.

You might like to use the blank template below to map one of the changes you want to make, which seems a bit challenging, using the Six Step Change Process.

Please consider doing this exercise with a qualified coach or a close friend, particularly Steps 3 and 4.

Step 1 – Current reality

Look back to the comments you made when you read chapter 2. How would you summarise your present relationship with time/your Purposeful Life?

Step 2 – Future vision

Look at the Purposeful Life diagram/vision you created at the end of chapter 7, your being plan from Chapter 11, your doing plan from Chapter 12 and the self versus others adjustment in chapter 13. Use these to identify a clear vision of you living your Purposeful Life, in 2 sections:

a) What you are doing in your Purposeful Life? How does it feel? What benefits you are experiencing?

b) Taking into account being as well as doing, what is your new relationship with time?

Step 3 and 4

Barriers – For each element in 2 above, write down in the first column below what is likely to stop you or slow you down in realising your future vision.

Sustainers – These are the beliefs, values and mindsets that keep the barriers in place. Use the ideas you collected during Chapters 4–6 for this. For each barrier ask yourself several times 'And what is keeping that in place?'. Write your answer in the sustainers column below (e.g. fear of looking stupid).

Barriers	Sustainers	Pro-active steps to overcome sustainers

Also at Step 4 list the benefits you are receiving as a result of your current behaviour e.g. 'variety'. If you want to take this benefit into your future, how might you continue to enjoy variety when you change to your desired lifestyle? Make a note of your answers and add them to Step 6.

'The day came when the risk to remain tight in a bud was more painful than the risk it took to blossom.'

Anaïs Nin

Step 5

Having completed Steps 1–4, and before completing your action plan, it's worth asking yourself:

a) What are the consequences of doing nothing to overcome these Sustainers and walking away from my vision of a Purposeful Life?

b) What are the consequences/benefits of achieving Step 2 and living my Purposeful Life?

c) What, if anything, do I need to be/do to become fully committed to change?

Step 6 – Commitment/Action plan

Now finalise your action plan including any support you may need from others and how you will go about getting it.

Main steps towards achieving my Purposeful Life, including actions from Step 4	Start date	Support needed	How I imagine I will feel when I am successful

In completing Step 6 you might wish to include tips you particularly liked when reading earlier chapters.

15 Keeping your momentum going

Break through to joy!

Dare to imagine that it might work!

What will life look like 6 months from now?

You have travelled a long way and have gone into some depth in designing your Purposeful Life. The challenge now is to keep going with implementing the action plan and to avoid slipping back into old behaviours.

There is some truth in the saying 'old habits die hard'. However, you may already have a successful strategy for changing behaviour and avoiding slipping back into old habits. If so, can you use it again? Further tips for maintaining change follow.

Make a picture

Use some coloured pens and draw a picture of yourself enjoying your Purposeful Life and display it as a reminder in one or more prominent places: on the wall in your office/study; inside the front cover of your diary/organiser; as a screen saver.

Find an object

Is there an object, or you could make an object, that represents your Purposeful Life? If so, put this object in a prominent place in your office or home.

Choose a mantra

Some of my business associates have written a mantra and pinned it up in their bathroom. They recite it to themselves first thing in the morning as they get ready for the day and last thing at night as they prepare for bed. The theory is that repeating a positive statement over and over again helps to erase an existing negative or unhelpful belief or thought.

Get a coach

The pro-forma action plan has a column headed 'support needed'. Support could come from one or more close friends and/or a professional coach. I would encourage you to get yourself a coach, particularly if you are wrestling with a self limiting belief or you anticipate that it will be difficult to shake off an old habit.

'Come what may,
Time and the hour run through the roughest day.'
Macbeth, Shakespeare

Thoughts from my contributors

Here are some thoughts from my contributors which may support you as you work through the rough bits:

> I sometimes use an affirmation like 'I always have enough time to do what needs to be done' or 'there is more than enough time in my day' and it always works.

> For enjoyable things, focus on the trees as well as the wood; for the negative ones, ignore the trees and concentrate on what's outside the wood!

Find comfort in realising that those who are more fortunate (in so many ways that we might find important) than we, also only have 24 hours per day at their disposal.

Ask yourself 'What is the best use of my time right now?'

When facing difficulties, ask yourself, 'How much will this matter in 6 months time?'

I never make instant decisions in response to urgent requests from others, and I live by the saying: 'If in doubt, leave it out!'

I express my appreciation to God every day for the life that He has given me – if I die tomorrow, I will have led a privileged and full life.

If you have to do something that you dislike, try to find pieces that are loveable about these things.

Longer being activities

Here are some longer mindfulness activities that you may find helpful when you feel you are in danger of losing touch with the self you want to become.

Breathing exercise – counting backwards.

Try doing this exercise last thing at night to help you go to sleep:
1. Inhale each breath slowly and deeply.
2. Feel the breath going deep into the body.
3. Number the first inhalation 10.
4. Number the first exhalation 10.
5. The next slow and deep inhalation is 9.
6. The corresponding exhalation is 9 and so on…. zzzz.

Breathing exercise – alternate nostrils

Alternate using the thumb and ring finger of one hand to cover your nostrils:

1. With the thumb of your left hand, close your left nostril and breathe in slowly and deeply through your right nostril.
2. Release your thumb and close the right nostril using the ring finger on your left hand, exhale slowly through your left nostril.
3. Keeping your ring finger in position inhale slowly and deeply through your left nostril.
4. Release your finger and use your thumb to close your left nostril. Exhale slowly through your right nostril.
5. Keep going for 10 minutes or so.

After the exercise:
(a) What changes have you noticed as a result of the exercise?
(b) Can this exercise be used to help stimulate the interplay between the left and right sides of the brain?
(c) What variations to the exercise would make it a richer experience, e.g. imagining each inhalation reaching the top of the head and the soles of the feet?

Now have a go at doing this exercise without using your thumb and finger.

A meditation exercise focusing on the breath

We focus on breathing partly because it is fundamental to life and also because changing your breathing can change your mental, emotional and physical states.

Choose a quiet place where you are unlikely to be interrupted for 15–20 minutes. Either sit comfortably in a straight backed chair with both feet placed firmly on the floor or lie on your back on the floor. Check that you are comfortable and warm enough.

Eliminate visual distractions by closing your eyes.

Breathe normally:
- Breathe in through your nose;
- Breathe out through your mouth.

Imagine that you are seated and looking out of a window at a clear blue sky:
- Occasionally clouds may pass by, some scurrying, some lingering.
- These clouds represent your thoughts. Be quite relaxed if some thoughts seem to want to linger.
- Concentrate on looking through the window and on your breathing.

With your eyes closed, mind very still, not thinking about anything at all, slowly begin to bring your mind to rest. Begin to withdraw from and ignore the world around you. Gradually turn your eyes inward and focus on your breath. Breathe in through your nose and out through your mouth. Soon you'll hear the sound of your own breathing. Be completely aware of the sound of your breathing. Be aware of the air streaming through your nostrils, filling your lungs, then being expelled through your lips. Visualise that stream of cold, fresh air being drawn in through your nostrils.

'See' it being drawn down, deep into your lungs. 'See' that stream of warm air being expelled through your lips. You are aware only of your breathing. Notice the sound, the rhythm, the temperature. Be completely absorbed by your breathing.

Having reached the stage where breathing is your foremost thought begin the breathing meditation [proceed with either A or B below]:

Option A

Count each breath as it leaves your body. Silently count 'one'. When the breath leaves, count 'two', then 'three' and 'four'. After 'four' begin at 'one' again and continue this silent count. *Hear* yourself saying each count. Imagine your own counting resounding in your head. (You do this without murmuring a sound). Count each breath: one, two, three, four, one two... until you become aware only of your counting. Don't think of what you're doing, or the relevance of it, or the meaning of the numbers. It has no meaning, no purpose other than counting four breaths and starting the count all over again. Every fibre of your being is involved in this one thing, and you are doing it completely.

Option B

With this variation on each inhalation you count silently to 4 and then with each exhalation you count silently to 4.

Go back to the square window frame. Picture this in your mind:

- **In breath** – Draw your eyes slowly up the left hand vertical side of the window frame as you count silently to 4.
- **Out breath** – Draw your eyes slowly (left to right) across the top horizontal frame as you count silently to 4.
- **In breath** – Draw your eyes slowly down the vertical right hand frame as you count silently to 4.
- **Out breath** – Draw your eyes slowly (right to left) across the bottom horizontal window frame as you count silently to 4.

Continue around the window frame for a further 5–15 minutes
Having become fluent in the above exercise, soften the corners of the window frame.

Conclusion of options A and B

When you are ready, in your own time slowly come out of this meditative state.

The four seasons of the year

How might you enjoy the annual rhythm of the four seasons in a single week or even a day?

	Annual Cycle	**Weekly Cycle**	**Daily Cycle**
Spring	Plan	———➤	———➤
Summer	Work	———➤	———➤
Autumn	Enjoy Rewards	———➤	———➤
Winter	Rest	———➤	———➤

Centring exercise to find your 'inner zone of excellence'

I learned the following exercise from Robert Dilts. It helps you to find your 'Inner Zone of Excellence'. It is reproduced, with permission, from pp.330–332 of *NLP II: The Next Generation* (co-authored with Judith DeLozier and Deborah Bacon Dilts). This exercise can be done on your own by following the 6 steps below:

1. Sit or stand in a comfortable position with both feet flat on the floor and your spine erect but relaxed (i.e., 'in your axis'). Check that your breathing is regular and from the belly. (Shallow, short or rapid breathing from the chest would indicate that you are in a stressed mode.)
2. Bring your attention to the soles of your feet (i.e., put your 'mind' into your feet). Become aware of the universe of sensations in the bottoms of your feet. Feel the surface of your heels, toes, arches and the balls of your feet.

3. Begin to expand your awareness to include the physical reality (the 3-dimensional space) of your feet and then move up through your lower legs, knees, thighs, pelvis and hips. Become aware of your belly centre and say to yourself, 'I am here'.

4. Continuing to stay aware of your lower body, move your awareness up through your solar plexus, spine, lungs, rib cage and chest. Focus on your heart centre and say to yourself, 'I am open'.

5. Expand your attention to move up through your shoulders, upper arms, elbows, lower arms, wrists, hands and fingers, and up through your neck, throat, face, skull and brain. Bring your awareness to the centre in your head, behind your eyes, and say to yourself, 'I am awake. I am alert and clear'.

6. Staying in contact with the ongoing physical sensations in your body and the three centres, become aware of all the space above you, reaching into the sky; all of the space below you, going into the centre of the Earth; all of the space to your left; all of the space to your right; all of the space behind you; all of the space in front of you. Say to yourself, 'I am ready'.

From Arawana

- Stand still with your eyes closed. Concentrate on the noises outside of you and try to count them. Concentrate on the distances: are they near or far off?

- When you feel all the noises are accounted for, start listening to the noises within. Can you hear – or rather feel – your own body? What's happening with your toes, your fingers, chest, face and crown?

- When you feel you've completely checked in, it's time to move. According to Arawana, the body has only two states: one is rest and the other is movement. Going from one state to the other is a huge feat which we inattentively do hundreds of times a day without a moment's thought. So the invitation is simple and overwhelming at the same time: see if you can go from the state of rest to the state of movement *consciously*.

- Concentrate, take just the one step and then stand still again. Strange as it may seem, this short but straightforward exercise does help to slow time down – even though it gets you strange looks from the neighbours if you do it too obviously whilst walking the dog.

For more information please see http://www.arawanahayashi.com

Quotations to help sustain being

My contributors sent me many quotations they love and that sustain them in their journeys. Thank you to the authors for writing such wonderful and helpful words, and to my contributors for signposting them for me. I have also added several of my own favourites.

What if the task is simply to unfold,
To become who you already are in your essential nature.
'The Dance', Oriah Mountain Dreamer

Time – neither to look forward nor back.
Time – to enjoy the sanctity of the present moment.
'Time', Mabel Holland

Live life forward and understand it backwards.
Anon

The power to make and keep commitments to ourselves is the essence of developing the basic habits of effectiveness.
Stephen R Covey

Quotations to help sustain doing

Boldness has genius, power and magic in it. Begin it now.
Johann Wolfgang von Goethe

Today I will act towards others as I would like them to act toward me.
I will not wait for tomorrow.
Guiding in Australia, Aug 1988

You never have time to do it right, but you always have time to do it again.
Bloch

Take time to dream – it hitches the soul to the stars
Guiding in Australia, Aug 1988

When it's over, I want to say: all my life
I was a bride married to amazement.
I was a bridegroom, taking the world into my arms.
'When Death Comes', Mary Oliver

Take benefit of five things:
Your youth before your old age,
Your health before your sickness,
Your wealth before your poverty,
Your free-time before your preoccupation,
And your life before your death.
Old Muslim saying

Happiness does not come from doing easy work but from the afterglow of satisfaction that comes after the achievement of a difficult task that demanded our best.
Theodore Rubin

Quotations for spiritual perspective

What lies before us and what lies behind us are small matters compared to what lies within us. And when we bring what is within us out into the world, miracles happen. In the end each of us will be judged by our standard of life, not by our standard of living: by our measure of giving, not by our measure of wealth; by our simple goodness not by our seeming greatness.
Gerard O'Donovan

Everybody can be great because anybody can serve. You don't have to have a college degree to serve. You don't have to make your subject and verb agree to serve. You only need a heart full of grace. A soul generated by love.
Dr Martin Luther King Jr

Our separation from each other is an optical illusion of consciousness.
Albert Einstein

The greatest unexplored territory in the world is the space between our ears.
Bill O'Brien

Be still before the Lord and wait patiently for Him, and do not fret when men succeed in their ways.
The Bible: Psalm 37 v 7

Non in tempore, sed cum tempore Deus creavit caelum et terra (Not in time, but with time God had created sky and land).
Augustinius

Teach us to number our days aright, that we may gain a heart of wisdom.
The Bible: Psalm 90:12

Then Jesus said.... do not worry about your life, what you will eat; or about your body, what you will wear. Life is more than food, and the body more than clothes.... Consider how the lilies grow. They do not labour or spin. Yet I tell you, not even Solomon in all his splendour was dressed like one of these. If that is how God clothes the grass of the field, which is here today, and tomorrow is thrown into the fire, how much more will he clothe you, O you of little faith!
The Bible: St Luke's Gospel, Chapter 12 vv 22-34

Nature does not hurry, yet everything is accomplished.
Lao Tzu, Chinese Taoist philosopher

A time to plant and a time to uproot
A time to tear down and a time to build
A time to search and a time to give up
A time to keep and a time to throw away.
The Bible: Ecclesiastes, Chapter 3 vv 2, 3, 6, 5, 7

Look to this Day
For it is life, the very life of life
In its brief course lie all the verities
And realities of your existence:
The bliss of growth
The glory of action
The splendour of beauty.
For yesterday is but a dream
And tomorrow is only a vision:
But today well-lived makes every yesterday
A dream of happiness
And every tomorrow a vision of hope.
Look well to this day.
'Look to this day', Rabindranath Tagore (My mother had this poem on her kitchen wall.)

And a quotation that is engraved on a paperweight on my desk:

> Things that matter most must never be at the mercy of things that
> matter least.
> *Goethe*

Taking a Purposeful Lives approach into the wider world

Using the Purposeful Lives ideas and process can help not just in your personal life, but also in a career and work context.

The next chapter shows how you can use the ideas from this book for career planning.

16 Career planning

As you have worked through the book you may well have asked yourself questions like 'Am I in the right job? What would I really like to do? How could I reshape my current role to align it more with my Purposeful Life?

If you are thinking of a career change either within your present organisation or moving to another job, then the exercises you completed earlier in the book will significantly reduce your preparation time in finding a job that you'd really love to do.

Earlier chapters in this book will help you to:
- Incorporate your unique strengths and talents into your CV so that you stand out from the rest of the crowd.
- Develop a powerful and authentic 'elevator speech' to use at networking events and when talking to friends.
- Answer interview questions like: 'Tell me about yourself?' or 'What motivates or inspires you?'

Three years ago a business friend and I set up a Job Club for unemployed people in our home town. With the help of another business friend, Louise Lloyd of Morley Lloyd Associates (www.morleylloyd.com), I created a Career Planning process and developed an 8 module programme which we work through each term.

This process chart is on the next page. The left hand column emphasises the importance of spending time at the beginning on some internal research. It is another example of an 'inside-out' approach to change.

Career planning in the context of a purposeful life

Adapt to new circumstances

Negotiate / choose

Maintaining contact and momentum

Preparation
- Marketing materials
- Tailoring CV
- Elevator speech
- Specific target research
- Networking
- Interview practice

Support systems
- Family & friends
- Exercise
- Leisure interest
- External coach
- Journaling

Refining my purpose

External research

What they want

What they offer

Career options

Internal research

What I offer:
- Uniqueness
- Skills/knowledge
- Core talents/strengths
- What inspires me

What I need:
- Money – min/max
- Geography
- Travel time
- To examine my limiting beliefs

What I want to match:
- Values
- Motivations
- Interests
- Size/type of organisation

Throughout: review, learn, adapt, grow

17 To the universe and beyond!

This book came into existence because of my dilemma with time – my feeling that time was flying past and that I wasn't making good use of it. The trigger for exploring my Purposeful Life was to make better use of time.

But as you begin to enjoy your new relationship with time, you can also begin exploring some provocative and challenging ideas.

Provocative ideas about time

- What if there was a completely different way of looking at time? What if we stepped outside all our current ideas about time and played with the idea that there are no limits to what we can do in relation to time?

- What if there is no single absolute TIME, but there is qualitative time – good time, fun time, nice time, great time, beautiful time – and in this we are already within eternity and multiple unfolding universes.

- We create our universe of time – it just depends on our ability to focus on what we want and it will become that for us. The better we become at living our lives the more it becomes the life we want and thus the time evolves to fulfil a balance between our expectations and our skills at realising our intentions.

- Time is a choice; it's like the soft footsteps that tip-toe through the night – be ready to embrace it and you will enjoy the most of it or be caught by it in a whirl of surprise and be overwhelmed by it.

- Live in a place of great expectations and develop your skills at making things happen. The two come together at that place called now, provided you are tuned to be there as it all happens. The you that needs to be there is the emotional you – seeing the beauty, fun, friendship, excitement and so on.

- Step through into the parallel universe of possibilities which is there all the time – it's almost as if 'you blink and you miss it', but it is more about stepping from the direct and looking on sideways. Then you are separate enough from the moment to be fully within it.

- Own your time and be responsible for it. Knowing what you know now, if you were to run a course on Time Leadership, what would be the key modules?

- Don't spend your life chasing riches and retirement; enjoy richness and fun throughout your life.

Questions for the journey

What does 'being content' mean? What would be my gains and losses if I were content with the present moment and accepted who I am?

What if I talked about life/work integration not life/work balance? What difference would that make to the way I view time?

What world would I find if I just stepped right outside this question of Time?

What would it be like to experience Eternity – right now?

What if it were possible to experience all the possibilities of the future, right now?

What if I were completely free to choose my response, in the moment, to any situation?

Contact our blog (www.purposefullives.com) to share your ideas with us and with other readers.

I have developed workshops, executive retreats and coaching programmes based on this book. Please get in touch for further information.

Happy travelling along your personal pathway.

Richard Fox
Richard@purposefullives.com
Twitter @purposefullives

Appendix

Biographical details with two stories about barriers to change and how to overcome them

Richard Fox

Brief biography

Richard aims to be a man of faith, hope and love. His unique talents and strengths cluster around him being an 'explorer', 'builder' and 'encourager'.

Richard had a fantastically rich and varied career in chartered accountancy – yes, chartered accountancy – reaching exalted heights as a partner in KPMG. He set up The Learning Corporation LLP, a pan European firm of executive coaches, mentors and training facilitators, 19 years ago.

Within the fields of personal and organisational development Richard is fascinated by the concepts of excellence and uniqueness. These have prompted him to become a Master NLP practitioner, a transformational ('generative') coach and to develop two new products, 'Purposeful Lives' and 'Purposeful Organisations'.

The golden thread running though Richard's work is leadership. He has trained well over 1,500 managers in personal leadership, building effective working relationships and in aspects of organisational leadership.

During his childhood he lived on the outskirts of Bristol and spent his leisure time enjoying the countryside, playing sports, Scouting and singing in the church choir. He can trace the development of his leadership skills back to his days as a patrol leader and head chorister.

Richard is the author of *The Fox Way* and enjoys designing and leading group walks, choral singing, the natural world and spending time with family and friends. He has known Heather Brown for 15 years and they have worked together on several client assignments.

Richard's struggle with using time intentionally

Step 1 – Describe the current state

I continue to work 6 days a week and notice that:
- I allow 40% of my time to be used on activities that I do well but which do not fully engage my unique talents and gifts.
- I do not spend enough time 'being' or enjoying the present moment.

Step 2 – Vision the desired state

I would like to:
(a) Focus my time on the Purposeful Lives side of our business.
(b) Delegate other types of client work to associates.
(c) Train myself to be totally present with my surroundings so that 'stopping to smell the roses' becomes second nature.
(d) Reduce my working hours to five x 8 hour days and take extra holidays.

Step 3 – List the barriers

Against (a) to (d) above:

(a)(i) My lack of knowledge in how to leverage social media to build the Purposeful Lives brand and business.

(b)(i) My love of variety of work.

(b)(ii) My over-willingness to say 'yes' to fee earning opportunities.

(b)(iii) My need to be seen as an expert.

(c) This is an interesting one! On the rare occasions that I do 'stand and stare' I notice that:

(i) Time's spinning top does slow down;

(ii) I enjoy the experience and feel at one with myself; and

(iii) My 'other than conscious mind' quietly continues to work on my business projects.

(d) As for (b) above.

Step 4 – Recognise the sustainers

The Sustainers keeping each Barrier in place:

(a) I have not yet created and implemented a new model of marketing Purposeful Lives that fully embraces social media because:

(i) I believe that Twitter is full of trivia.

(ii) I believe I need to understand the connections between Twitter, LinkedIn, www.purposefullives.com and income generation before I can delegate marketing activities to others.

(b)(i) I love variety of work. Intellectually, I know that there is an enormous variety of content within the scope of Purposeful Lives. The blocker is probably due to my lack of belief in how quickly this product can generate income.

(b)(ii) Deep down a teenage fear of poverty fuels a driver for personal achievement. I have let go of some of the resulting work addiction; however, 'old habits die hard'.

(b)(iii) I have not yet realised that I already am an expert in Purposeful Lives.

(c) Until I overcome the addiction to work, the balance of my time will continue to weigh heavily towards 'doing' to the detriment of 'being'.

(d) As for (b)(ii).

Step 5 – List the consequences of current behaviour/ desired state

(a) Of continuing my current behaviour (Step 1).

My time will continue to whizz by and I will not find time to implement ideas in this book. I will not be living my life to the full. I want to achieve Step 2 as I do not want to continue bouncing cheques on myself.

(b) Living my desired state (Step 2).

I will be living a balanced life way beyond the scope of traditional time management books. I will be using my talents and gifts more fully. I will be a 'human becoming' more than a 'human doing'.

Step 6 – Make commitments to mindset and first action steps

1. Work with my coach to package the Purposeful Lives product for (a) use within organisations; and (b) personal clients. This will feed my need to be seen as an expert. Remember to maximise 'variety' within Purposeful Lives.

2. Work with an expert in social media on Step 4(a) above to create a marketing/communications plan (I have sufficient cash reserves to give me time to build up this business).

3. Commission a research assistant to review all our materials on Purposeful Lives and Stop Time's Spinning Top and create a programme of blogs and tweets.

4. Identify and delegate routine fee-earning work to associates.

5. Ask a close friend to hold me accountable to take one week's holiday each term.

6. Work with my coach on (i) reducing my working hours; (ii) implementing some of the ideas in my book so I rebalance my time between being v doing and present v future.
7. Set a date when I will celebrate progress made with the above.

Heather Brown

Brief biography

The theme of Heather's career has been helping individuals and teams to achieve their potential. She started work in teaching, then worked as an outdoor instructor on management development programmes in Australia, and eventually went indoors to work on the Telstra (a major telecoms company) MBA programme. Since her return to the UK she has worked in all branches of management development, from consultancy, programme design and delivery to coaching and supporting individuals.

More recently she has been involved in executive coaching, talent and career management, designing and facilitating team effectiveness and change management workshops. Her present projects include co-designing and teaching on a Masters in Professional Development, co-facilitating a major regional leadership programme, and leading a 7 year change project to develop a CPD structure and culture for the Outdoor Sector.

Heather's aim is to integrate head, heart and body in her own life and in her work; she runs a practice in Shiatsu (Japanese clothed massage) and uses bodywork and Qi Gong in her coaching when clients are up for it!

Heather's struggle with time

I was very impressed by one poem sent to Richard - Oriah Mountain Dreamer's 'What If?' The phrases from the poem which particularly struck me were:

> What if becoming who and what we truly are happens not through striving and trying,
> But by recognising and receiving the people and places and practices
> That are for us the warmth of encouragement we need to unfold?
> How would this shape the choices you make about how to spend today?

Step 1 – Describe current behaviour and reality

I am a planner; I make lists, I fill my days with activity, and when I have a moment, I read improving books, take exercise, try to meditate (mostly with little success!). I want everything in life to be organised and without surprises, so that the world will stand still to give me time to contemplate, to be at peace without feeling that I should be doing something productive, not wasting time. And I never seem to get on top of it all; there is always something else to do!

I need to take responsibility for this feeling that I must always be doing something 'useful', (rather than blaming my parents, school, religious education or whatever). So what am I scared will happen, if I stop? Some part of me believes that:

1) I will not find what I'm looking for (that my life will be over before I find it, if I don't spend every minute searching).
2) That people will criticise me for being self-centred in this search, unless I make it 'hard work' and unless I spend all the rest of my time serving others.

Step 2 – Vision the desired state

Oriah's poem implies to me that it might be possible to live in a place where I could stop trying and trust that what I need/seek will be given to me. So let me dare to imagine this fully.

I meditate or do yoga or Qi Gong, not focusing on how long it's taking or whether I'm doing it right, but receiving what each movement and moment has to offer me, rather than trying to THINK about what I should be getting out of it, trying to conjure a result, to make IT happen (IT being enlightenment, release, peace, magic, happiness, connectedness).

I am surrounded by friends whom I love, and who show me that they love me. I can receive gifts of care from them without feeling I need immediately to rouse myself to give something back; knowing that a time will come where it will be right for me to care for them as they have cared for me. I feel the warmth of encouragement, and trust that doing this is not only what is best for me, but that it will enable me to make my best contribution to the universe.

Step 3 – List the barriers to achieving this vision

My biggest Barrier is thinking – trying to nut out the meaning of the universe. Mentally I know I'm not going to find it, but the only alternative stance seems to be to stop trying, to become fatalistic.

Fatalism – giving up any idea of connection with something bigger than me, burying my head in the sand, living through my emotions and being at the prey of them	AS OPPOSED TO	Seeking by thinking – imagining the big ideas, using my intellect, what I'm good at

The other main barrier is feeling worthy to receive without immediately giving. I don't know what else to say about that at this precise moment!

Step 4 – Recognise the sustainers of the barriers (beliefs, values and drivers)

Thinking – I am scared to stop thinking; I am known as someone who thinks, my job means that I am paid to think. If I stopped thinking there would be emptiness, and I would no longer be in control of how long it might take for an answer to appear – I could be waiting for ever.

Worthiness to receive – feeling worthy to receive feels like selfishness.

Step 5 – List the consequences of (a) current reality and (b) desired vision

Thinking – If I keep on thinking in a way which is focussed on finding an answer, I will worry/think myself into illness because there is no answer in this life to the question I ask, namely, what is the meaning of the universe?

If I can find a third stance, which is not trying to either find the answer to the universe or becoming totally fatalistic, perhaps I can:

- Rest and trust in the mystery, enjoying the journey?
- Use my intellect to ask better questions, and trust that the answer will come when it's ready?

Feeling worthy to receive. If I keep on feeling I am not worthy to receive, then I cut myself off from receiving love in order to avoid feeling abandoned. If I continue to cut myself off, then I will be abandoned much more definitively than if I dare to risk engagement.

If I recognise that I can build a bank of giving credit, it will help me believe that I have more of a right to receive. If I practise receiving, engaging, and each time I feel guilty, remind myself that I have the right to receive, then perhaps I can start to trust that I don't have to calculate the bank of credit exactly, and I can rest and enjoy the support and encouragement around me.

That will make a difference to the choices I will make about how to spend today. Rather than the compulsion to seek 'the answer', I will be led by touching base with my purpose. This will help me be more peaceful, help me feel more useful to others, and release me from the feeling that I never have enough time.

Step 6 – Commitment

So the first steps to my commitments are:
1. On a daily basis, to change my question 'what's the answer to the universe', to 'why am I here?' and 'What is it most useful to the universe for me to do at this moment?' and wait quietly for guidance.
2. To practise giving, to engage, and to practise receiving. Each time I feel guilty, to remind myself that I have the right to receive.
3. To hear the encouragement that others give me.
4. To focus on unfolding.

Index